# MILTON'S MARILYN

# MILTON'S MARILYN

## The Photographs of Milton H. Greene

Written by James Kotsilibas-Davis
Directed by Joshua Greene

SCHIRMER/MOSEL

MOSS RUNN, LTD.

The publishers are grateful to Joshua and Anthony Greene, who provided the photographs reproduced in this book from their private collection. All of the photos, with the exception of a few family shots, unless otherwise stated, are by Milton H. Greene and his studio.

Frontispiece: This striking portrait emerged from Marilyn Monroe's first sitting with Milton H. Greene at the Twentieth Century-Fox portrait studio in Hollywood in September 1953 for the Christmas edition of *Look*.

Distributed in the USA by Moss Runn, Ltd.
4065 Hollis Street, Emeryville, CA 94608
Contact: Heather Cameron (510) 658-3453, x247

Design: Beda Achermann and Schirmer/Mosel
Lithos: O.R.T. Kirchner GmbH, Berlin
Typesetting: Typ-O-Graph, Munich
Printing and binding: Appl, Wemding

ISBN 0-9646873-3-X (Moss Runn edition)
A Schirmer/Mosel production

# ACKNOWLEDGMENTS

I would like to thank all for going back, back, back in time to focus on a period of five years, forty years ago. First, thanks to Milton for sticking me in a darkroom at thirteen and teaching me to "see" and to understand all that's important is "how it looks …"

To my mom Amy for wholeheartedly leading the way in many areas of this production, and to my younger brother Anthony, whose spirit, imagination, and fire always motivate me.

To Inez "Kitty" Owens, my second mother, who raised me and took care of all of us including Marilyn. To Jay Kanter, who has always been there with words of guidance. Pat Newcomb for her fond recollections of Milton. To Don Murray, Judy Balaban Quine, Michael Korda, Eileen Heckart, John Springer, Joyce Saffir, Marvin Paige, Phillip Kunhardt, and Jesse Rand for their interviews.

May this also be a tribute to Jule Styne, Clyde and Inez Owens who shared their memories but passed away during the making of this book and each in their own way were very special and dear to the Greene family.

A deep appreciation to James Kotsilibas-Davis from the bottom of my heart for clearing his desk while in the throws of the Gish sisters. To Liz Smith for always being so supportive and helping Anthony, Milton, and Marilyn. Special thanks to Freedman Greene Productions for allowing us to quote from interviews with Susan Strasberg, David Brown, and Allan "Whitey" Snyder.

On a more technical side, to Gordon Freedman who introduced me to the world of *Adobe Photoshop*, which is what made the restoration of the images in this book possible. To Mac Holbert and the Nash Editions Team for a glimpse of the digital future. To Carol Color Lab, the most loyal and trustworthy photo lab in New York City, I love you. To GP Color Online Systems in Los Angeles, and Barclay Cook for his old school black and white darkroom, where I can still touch photography. My special thanks to Miki Denhoff, who said in her own matter of fact voice, "You know, Joshua, a book on Milton should start with a family album so people understand who he really was." I must thank my favorite sister-in-law Robin Greene for her eternal optimism and extraordinary driving skills in Los Angeles. To both Anne Druba and Anna Womack for the little things that matter greatly like the communications between Lothar and myself. To Yvette de Botton for transcribing Jim's interviews and working beyond the call of duty to computerize the final manuscript. To Victor Disuvero and Barbara Windom for my time in Santa Fe, where it became apparent that the talker in me needed to become the author of this introduction. To Toula Polygalaktos for her editorial corrections. To Mary Emmerling, who has been most understanding in allowing me to work on this project while we have had two books of our own to complete.

To Sheila Chefetz for being an example that hard work and patience is always rewarded. To Soffie Kage, who has always shown me unconditional love and reminded me to "keep the integrity in the art and in life." To Joe Eula, a great artist, who was Milton's partner and longtime friend, you are my strongest living connection to Milti and always steer me when I get off track. Finally to Lothar Schirmer, your love for photography and high standards in publishing are rare in today's marketplace. I am honored to be part of your family. Also to Charlie Winton for his straight-forward and open style of business which made this English text version possible.

A special thanks to my meditation master for bestowing grace in my life and teaching me to strive for compassion at all times.

*Joshua Greene*
August 1995

# INTRODUCTION

When I think of New York in the '50s, I hear that empty sax in an L.C. Alley, wet streets, smoke in the air, and all types of people hustling their ideas and dreams.

480 Lexington Avenue was an old-fashioned eleven story office building from the turn of the century surrounded by great old hotels like the Park Lane, Marquery and the Waldorf Astoria two blocks away. It was connected to Grand Central Station by a vaulted arcade from Lexington to Park Avenue. Miltons's top-floor studio had a balcony all around, a cat burglar's dream. With twenty-foot ceilings and windows to the floor which swung open, it was more like being in Rome than in New York.

Milton Greengold was fifth of five children of a Russian immigrant tailor. They lived out in Sheepshead Bay, New York.

In his only photography course at Abraham Lincoln High School, he was failed for purposely reticulating the film, which adds grain and texture to an image, a technique commonly used today.

At seventeen he began assisting a *Life* photographer, Eliot Elisofon, among others, and soon after dropped the "gold" from his name.

Milton learned the business quickly. He shot for catalog houses and public relations firms and he went into partnership with the technical photo wizard, Marty Bauman.

Bauman/Greene Studio did everything: cars, washers, dryers, bras, furs—mostly advertising. Milton leaned more towards people than items. He missed the spontaneity of grabbing a moment of beauty and left Marty to become a fashion photographer at Macy's.

Milton, who took his work very seriously, was shooting late one night alone at the store. Someone came knocking on the locked door. Milton went to answer it and denied the insistent gentleman entry, only to find out the next day that the man at the door was Mr. Macy and Milton was fired.

His love of women and beauty led him deeper into fashion, where his non-conforming style of working with whatever was around gave him great versatility for the editorials. Magazines were it, top of the roost, they had the audience …

Milton was shy, but loved music and people, and at night after the building would vacate, he would let some jazz musician friends—Max Roach, Miles Davis, Gene Krupa, and Dizzy Gillespie—come to "the studio" and "jam".

This was an innocent time when Marlene Dietrich, Frank Sinatra, Audrey Hepburn, Cary Grant, Sammy Davis, Ava Gardner, Elizabeth Taylor, Norman Norell, or Lauren Bacall might find each other over at "480 Lex", for an afternoon lunch Italian peasant style or cocktails overlooking the city at night while diggin' on some licks.

Milti, as he was known to some, had a childlike playfulness. This sensitivity guided his rapport so that his subjects never sensed the camera. His "eye", following the graceful lines of fashion and mixed with his true gift, "timing", preserved moments of uncommon beauty.

Milton was hot and swingin' as a freelance photographer. He did assignments for *Life,* was under contract with *Look* and supported a full roster of advertising accounts.

It was 1953, New York City was supporting some great photographers, Irving Penn, Richard Avedon, Gordon Parks, Diane Arbus, Elliott Erwitt, Gjon Mili, Alfred Eisenstaedt, Cornell Capa and Milton. These spontaneous artists set new standards and laid the foundation for today's work. This was also the year that long-time friend Fleur Cowles, editor-in-chief at *Look,* asked Milton to go to Los Angeles to shoot Marilyn Monroe for their November holiday issue, and that story is in the following pages.

Milton and Joe Eula would say to me all my life, "if it doesn't look right, change it," "know when to leave it alone" and "imperfection is perfection." They also taught me to love everything which presented itself in balance—nature, painting, sculpture, architecture, and photography.

When Milton printed he would use strong developers and diffuse the grain with old silk stockings. As simple as this was it created a very striking and personal effect to his black and white work which became his signature. We used this technique to print all of Milton's black and white images.

These color images, which were mostly unusable due to improper storage and the passage of time, have now been restored through *Adobe Photoshop* and the digital technology of today. This technology makes it possible to have bold and beautiful color reproductions for the collectors and admirers of art photography.

Lothar Schirmer has been after this book since 1984 and though its conception has changed, the body of that work is here. Milton never felt comfortable exploiting Marilyn, and so to honor his nature, we have specifically tried to capture their side of the story.

After years of drifting like a little boat lost at sea, I feel that I've reached land. This book is a vision I have had for some time. Although so many of Milton's photographs of Marilyn have become synonymous with her image it was a revelation to me how many more images existed. I hope this will be the beginning of bringing Milton's work to a new audience for photography.

The love and respect that I have for my father as a person and as an artist is the driving force behind orchestrating this book project. With the utmost respect to all involved, I thank you for your guidance, your lessons and your love.

This one is for you Milti …

*Joshua Greene*

# CONTENTS

James Kotsilibas-Davis

# MILTON AND MARILYN

A Collaboration

The day after Marilyn's thirtieth birthday, she and Milton (with the briefcases) arrived at Idlewild airport, New York, after completing the shooting of *Bus Stop*. Photo: UPI.

# FADE IN

Marilyn loved the still camera. The still camera reflected that love. Never was it more evident than in the five-year collaboration with Milton Greene. So many Monroe books have materialized since her death with so many images, so many claims of intimacy that it seems trite to say something special happened with a particular photographer. But look, just look at these pictures culled from nearly fifty sittings—the gypsy in the window, the scrubbed graduate, the pool nymph, the wistful ballerina—look and say there is not something singular about this exchange. Look and say the man behind the lens does not emerge as vividly as the woman in front of it.

Lovers? Marilyn had lots of lovers. She liked making love. So did he. But this was a threesome: Marilyn, Milton, and the camera. "Milton was never in love with Marilyn," asserted their friend Jule Styne. "He loved the face in the lens." What happened between them transcended sex.

Marilyn sits patiently and seemingly relaxed as make-up is applied for her second sitting with Milton in 1953.

"He understood her better than anybody and she understood him better than anybody," states Amy Greene Andrews, Milton's wife of thirty-two years. "Many times people would say to me, 'Oh, how can you have her in your house, in your life blah, blah, blah?' I trusted her completely. As a woman, I trusted her. In the Spoto book and this book and that book Milton and Marilyn were having an affair. Bullshit! They didn't need to go to bed and bang. That wasn't important to them. They had their own credentials and they had their own sphere and no one else got in there."

"Whether or not he fucked her, I think Milton genuinely liked Marilyn," adds author Michael Korda. "He didn't at all exploit her and they had a great deal in common. They both had difficult and needy childhoods. They were both terribly needy for human emotion, warmth, and companionship. They were both rather quiet, shy, introspective people with a tough undercore of greed and ambition. Milton and Marilyn got along in a very relaxed, easy-going way, which she didn't with most people, which explains why she went with Milton into the movies and why his photographs of her are better than anybody else's."

The auspicious meeting of Marilyn Monroe and Milton H. Greene took place in August 1953. Some sources claim that they met in Hollywood in 1949, while he was on assignment for *Life.* Supposedly they shacked up for ten days at the Chateau Marmont, then parted without a picture being taken. The former allegation is plausible, the latter preposterous. "Milton wouldn't even go to the bathroom without his camera," says Amy, "so how could that meeting have taken place? He never mentioned such a thing to anyone."

Milton always told Amy and, among others, his friends Korda and Norman Mailer that they met on a later *Look* assignment. "I would take Milton's word for that," says Korda.

Why belabor this issue? Because it typifies the rampant mythology surrounding every aspect of Marilyn's life: Just stretch the truth a bit and spice up the story. Regarding this backwash of speculation, we have aimed in these pages for testimony from participants, rather than conjecture from spectators. Joe Eula, the artist who became Milton's friend and partner, rankles at the suggestion of an earlier meeting. As to a telegram allegedly confirming it, uncovered by Johanna Thorman, Milton's part-time companion at the time of his death in 1985: "Absolutely a lie, lie, lie! Some telegram—I don't know who ever got that jerked-off dream—it's totally untrue. Milton never met Marilyn until 1953 when he went out there to do a story for *Look* magazine. Johanna—just take a look at her. What kind of validity would you ever put behind that asshole?"

The truth behind the relationship of Milton Greene and Marilyn Monroe rests in the photographs. The lens of a great photographer does not lie. What emerged from those sittings is affirmation and courage for new beginnings, a golden period that yielded a hundred deathless images and two memorable films. What followed from the exigency of fate and character does not diminish them.

# THE HOT SHOT

As Head of Magazine Publicity for Twentieth Century-Fox in the early '50s, John Springer arranged most of the photo shoots. He describes what obtaining the services of Milton Greene meant to the studio: "Any star I had I would desperately try to get photographed by Milton Greene, because that was always a layout in *Life* or a layout in *Look* or something of importance. He was right at the top, in that top echelon of photographers who could get a star exposed most importantly in one of the great magazines. Milton was a star himself."

A stellar career in photography became more accessible to a poor Russian Jew from Brooklyn after World War II had jumbled society. It is unlikely that the United States will ever again see the like of that post-war generation. You were the biggest winner in the world if you were in motion. Who could stop you? It was there for the taking. There was a group of artistic young men around New York ready to take it. They were not quite painters or writers or composers, but they were ambitious, bright and, above all, creative. They became photographers.

Milton Greengold fell in love with photography as a boy. While attending high school in Brooklyn he apprenticed with Martin Bauman in Manhattan, learning quickly the technical skills Bauman was noted for. The boy's energy and instinctive "eye," that rare gift of photographic foresight, led Bauman to offer him a partnership. Before Milton reached his mid-twenties he had joined that select group of photographers working for the big picture magazines—*Life, Look, Colliers, Vogue, Harper's Bazaar*—whose power and popularity swelled in the decade after the war until television overtook them.

They rode the crest of that "top echelon" of so-called fashion photographers: Irving Penn, Richard Avedon, Bert Stern, and particularly Milton H. Greene. (The "H.", added as an inside joke when the family name was shortened, stood for Hawthorne.) "He was considered the biggest hot shot, the bright star," Eula insists. "Everyone always says it was Marilyn. It was *Life* that gave Milton the key to the whole goddamned kingdom. They gave him all those covers when a cover really meant something.

Everybody at that time wanted to be on the cover of *Life*."

Milton's specialty was not fashion, really, it had much more to do with entertainment. But Sally Kirkland, *Life*'s dynamic fashion editor, frequently lured him into her realm for an extraordinary array of essays. "She'd just send us down to the Virgin Islands or some place with a bag of clothing, without even an editor, and we'd come back with four covers," says Eula.

His services were always amply rewarded. He drove a hard bargain. According to Philippe Halsman, another colleague, "Milton picked up every photographer and put him in the big money category." He was an artist, but he was nobody's fool.

"Milton came from pretty humble beginnings, so when he started making money he was always afraid of being broke," recalls his friend, talent manager Jesse Rand. "Milton spent, but he watched what he spent, and when it came to business he was sharp. He made a deal. If you wanted Milton Greene's services, *boy* … "

Rand remembers being in Milton's studio when an account executive from one of the big advertising agencies blustered in. After some lively discussion, Rand heard Milton say, "Five-thousand dollars."

"Five-thousand dollars!" cried the agency man. "You told me twenty-five hundred a couple of months ago."

"Yeah, but you went to another guy who was cheaper, and now that the other guy fucked up you're coming back to me. I want five thousand."

"You're crazy."

"No. I'm Milton Greene." So Milton Greene got the five thousand to take a picture of a tube of toothpaste. But it was not just greed with him. It was pride.

Rand, who managed Sammy Davis Jr., asked Milton to do the cover for his Decca Records album. "They can't afford me," Milton told him. "That's why I don't do album covers."

"Tell you what," Rand hedged, "I'll get them to give you one of those new stereos just out and a hundred albums, whatever you want, and I'll put you on the promotional mailing list … "

"You mean you want me to take the picture for nothin'?"

"For nothin'."

"I'll do it."

Milton used to espouse a sort of "Magnificent Obsession" theory of reciprocation: "Come on, let's face it, we all plug into each other. If somebody wants something from me, fine, then I expect something from somebody else." Something other than a new stereo and a great picture came out of that album cover. Besides attracting lucrative assignments from record companies, it cemented life-long friendships with Rand and Davis.

It started back in 1952, when Rand wanted to get his client into one of the big magazines, which in those days, he says, were not prone to featuring "Negroes." A friend in public relations had an idea: "There's a photographer in town who has carte blanche with the big magazines. Fleur Cowles at *Look* loves him. *Life* loves him. He's a hell of a photographer and has a great rap. Give him a call." Rand called and made an appointment to see Milton Greene.

"I come into this fabulous studio, fabulous penthouse with a cathedral ceiling and a balcony all around," Rand relates, "and I see this guy all dressed in black—black turtleneck sweater, black linen jacket, black sneakers." (Milton had dozens of replicas of that basic black outfit made for him in Rome; it became his uniform.)

"Your name Jessie?" he asked.

"No, Jesse," Rand corrected.

"Oh, I'm Milton. I'll see you in a minute." He rushed off and returned twenty minutes later. "Talk to me," he said. His direct delivery, a sort of staccato Brooklynese, belied years of painstaking practice to overcome childhood stuttering.

Rand invited him to see Sammy Davis Jr. perform at the Copacabana. The multi-talented entertainer so impressed Milton he did a layout "on spec." But despite his clout—and he fought for the story all the way up the chain of command to Henry Luce—*Life* would not print it.

That "fabulous" studio, at 480 Lexington Avenue, perched propitiously beside the offices of Condé Nast publications in the Graybar Building next door. There was rough magic in that vast space surrounded by a crenelated loggia where Milton could pose his subjects or practice his fly-fishing. "It was a strange, romantic place with lights popping, wonderful-looking models and makeup people running around," recalls Phil Kunhardt, a *Life* assistant managing editor, who often assigned and laid out Milton's stories. Yet within that frenetic space Kunhardt discerned a calm, creative center: "Milton went about his photography in a strong, gentle way. He never raised his voice. He always dealt with his subjects on a quiet basis, yet managed to get so much out of them."

"Some photographers either went overboard with 'lovey ... honey ... ' or maintained an aloofness," adds John Springer. "Milton had a way of making a star feel very comfortable, very relaxed, and someone like Marilyn had to feel cared for, had to feel relaxed."

"You mustn't particularize that," warns Michael Korda, "because Milton had the same relationship with many subjects. I saw him with Judy Garland. He was very, very good with all people, but particularly with needy women. He was soft spoken, kind and decent to them. He was admiring. He was supportive and positive. He reinforced their best feelings about themselves. He was fond of Judy, and Judy, who had been brutalized by everybody including Sid Luft, responded very well to Milton, which is why his photographs of her are so special."

Milton was intense but terribly shy, a kind of classy John Garfield. With his gentle manner, his darkly sensual good looks and his dazzling smile he could disarm anyone, needy or not. He was the vulnerable little boy everyone wanted to tell it all to, and consequently they would bare their souls for his camera. All you had to do was look at the photographs the next day. You saw yourself as you had never seen yourself before—even Marlene Dietrich felt that way, and she did not have an insecure bone in her body.

She stormed into the studio like gangbusters, not to be fooled, not to be trifled with. She would do this *Life* sitting only because of the "grandmother angle," but he could not take a picture unless he gave her absolute approval over anything that would run. She took over. She insisted that the light be placed where she knew it would be best for her. She knew it all. She had learned it from her mentor, Josef von Sternberg. "Well, we'll try it this way and we'll try it that way and we'll make a compromise," soothed Milton, pacifying Dietrich and never changing a thing.

The next day, she came in and approved practically everything. She was ecstatic. Milton could do no wrong after that, particularly when *Life* put her on the cover. "You must have a rubber lens," she told him. "You went around corners to get what you wanted."

He had a way with women. Not that it limited him. Cary Grant always said that Milton's pictures were the best ever taken of him, and backed it up by making Milton color consultant on his film *That Touch of Mink*. But, no doubt about it, something special emerged when he photographed women. "Richard Avedon once told me, 'Milton is the greatest photographer of women I've ever met,'" claimed Jule Styne. "When one of Milton's Marilyn sittings came out, he said, 'Jeez, he's unbelievable. He tells the whole story. It's more than a fine picture.'"

The artist had an edge—depressive, introverted and moody. "Russian gloom," Amy called it, and it could be quite charming until, in his last years, it engulfed him. "There was something profoundly sad about Milton," observes Judy Balaban Quine. "I don't mean pitiful; I mean sad, a pervasive sense of sadness like a grieving thing. It may have been part of what gave him that subtext with Marilyn."

That "subtext" is an essential aspect of Milton. Quine, now an author, discerned it as the wife of Jay Kanter, Milton and Marilyn's agent during the turbulent years of Marilyn Monroe Productions. He often seemed not to be present in the text of the moment, but in a subtext. "Talking to Milton," says actress Phyllis Newman, "was like looking at an abstract painting." He would initiate a conversation, usually something he wanted to know about. Everybody would be contributing, exchanging ideas, and he would be long gone.

"He had taken the A train out in another direction," Quine continues, "leaving you all there on the platform not knowing the schedule. In a way you thought it was rude, but in another way I think it was all a part of Milton's creative mechanism. He went to places in his head to get into the subtext and end up in the studio. The subtext planned what he needed to lead him down this tunnel to the light at the end of the lens. Milton's soul lived in the camera."

His heart lived in the country. When he was not in the studio he hightailed it to the rustic vaulted-ceilinged retreat he had created from an old barn in Weston, Connecticut. He loved playing country squire with the tractor and the jeep and the big boat for bluefishing. He entertained, but his cronies and his women took a backseat to country living.

"Milton didn't like the social element he was living in in New York," recalled Styne. "It was the other fellow, Dick Avedon, who adapted to it and benefited from it. Milton didn't go with it for some reason." He was shrewd enough, however, to know his business required social contact. At parties he never stayed with people he already knew, but mingled with the new ones. He attracted a kind of traveling court which gathered for drinks at the studio in the evening and spent weekends in Weston. Celebrities he took as a matter of course. "Come on, we're going to a party at Judy and Jay Kanters'," he told Jesse Rand.

"Now we ring the door bell and who the hell answers the door but Marlon Brando?" Rand marvels.

"I'll never forget it. But to Milton this is just a client of Jay's he pals around with. He even used to screw up his name, always called him 'Marly Brandy.'"

Milton's New York associations would prove to be propitious when Marilyn and the movies beckoned. His friend Jay Kanter, a Hollywood agent in MCA's New York office, married Judy Balaban, daughter of the founder of the Balaban & Katz theater chain who became head of Paramount. All these second-generation Hollywood children—Jean Stein, Suzy Zanuck, Barbara Warner, Judy Goetz—held court at Danny's Hideaway and Milton ran with them. When he would go out to Hollywood the Jules Stein family welcomed him, the Zanucks, Barney Balaban. Milton had everyone.

He also had someone who loved that life and orchestrated it for him. "I think for him," Judy Quine continues, "all the stuff that existed out there that Amy managed and kind of planned and arranged was all somewhat a facilitation of Milton's subtext. It allowed his subtext to become more real than it would have been had it just stayed in his head."

"Your talent gets us in the door," Amy cautioned, "but once we're in we better have something to talk about or they won't ask us back."

"You talk," Milton told her.

Cuban-born Amy Franco has the looks of a Meissen muse and the guts of an Amazon. Fair and petite, with a nose plastic surgeons take millions to duplicate, she is outspoken and supremely confident. When her parents divorced before her sixth birthday, she was sent away to a convent school. As a teenager she lived on Manhattan's upper West Side with her mother, where she spent every possible minute at the movies, living the movies. Her first job was ushering at the Shubert Theater during the long run of *Bloomer Girl*. She became what in those days was called a cover girl, posing for the likes of Richard Avedon. She even had an appointment to show her book to Milton Greene for an ad he was shooting, but he was late and she left. No one kept Amy Franco waiting. Her agency set up another appointment with Milton Greene a couple of months later, but someone proposed marriage to her over a table at 21 that day. She refused the offer, but in the wake of her first proposal she completely forgot her "go see" at Bauman-Greene.

They finally met before he left to cover the Paris couture collections for *Life*. He and David Haft, whom she dated occasionally, threw a big farewell party at Milton's studio. Nicky Hilton started chasing her around when she arrived, so she said, "Hello, Milton Greene/Goodbye, Milton Greene" and bolted.

Stories about Milton Greene flew around the fashion world that summer of 1952. All the guys were in awe of him, all the women had crushes on him. He was the hero, doing all the things they only dreamed about. When he and the beautiful model Nelly Nyad quit Paris for a passionate fling in Spain, the rich old man who kept her tracked them with a ready revolver. It was all so romantic.

In Venice he was invited on the yacht of Arturo Lopez Wilshire, one of the world's richest men with a fortune built on guanaco droppings. When Milton, looking sleek in his usual black, boarded the yacht, the host zeroed in on him. Milton, used to being propositioned, thought he could handle it. But this was a boat and Wilshire was persistent. Running out of diversionary tactics, he noticed in desperation his host's magnificent cufflinks.

"Those are wonderful, really great," Milton hedged. "Tiffany ... Cartier ... Van Cleef & Arpels?"

Wilshire smiled and shook his head: "Cellini."

Something, perhaps pride in his possessions, diverted the hunter and the quarry slipped away. Milton loved telling that story.

Meanwhile, bilingual Amy became head of the Spanish-American Shop at Lord & Taylor. Realizing that she was too small to go very far as a model, she had joined their training program to become a buyer. That autumn she had a movie date with David Haft, who owned Swansdown, a big Seventh Avenue company. They were on their way to see *Limelight*, when Milton Greene jumped out of a cab on Fifth Avenue and ran past them toward the Savoy Plaza.

"Hey, what are you doing here?" Haft called.

"I'm going up to Nelly. I have to pay her hotel bill." When Haft asked if he had enough money, Milton pulled out a wad of bills.

"Are you crazy?" scolded Amy. "Don't flash that money in the middle of Fifth Avenue. You're going to get killed." He looked at her, wondering where the hell this tiny person was coming from. "You've got enough money there to choke a horse. Put it in your pocket." He put it in his pocket and went into the hotel, looking back over his shoulder at this curious creature.

A couple of months later on another date with Haft, Amy stopped at his apartment while he changed. "As long as we're going down to Chinatown for dinner, I've invited Milton Greene," Haft said. "Do you mind?"

"Wait a minute!" Amy snapped. "I don't have a date with Milton Greene. I have a date with you."

"Yeah, but he's carrying a big torch for Nelly and it's getting to him. Be kind."

"Oh, all right," she agreed reluctantly. Haft asked her to make the guest a drink when he arrived and went in to shower and change. The doorbell rang and she let Milton Greene in.

"Now it's just Milton and Amy," she relates. "He's sitting on one side of the fireplace; I'm sitting on the other. We begin to talk. At that point in time I couldn't care less if David Haft went down the drain, because I fell in love with Milton and he fell in love with me. And I knew that was it." He asked where he could call her. She told him, but he did not call. She sent him a Christmas card. He called.

"I got your card," he said. "Would you like to come up to Connecticut? I have a place there."

"Well, I don't usually go away on weekends." Amy was twenty at the time, Milton ten years older.

"You can have your own bedroom." ("Yeah, right: 'You can have your own bedroom,'" Amy mocks forty years later.) He picked her up, off they went, and that did it. She never left.

The following summer Amy became pregnant: "I went to Milton—you know, Miss Uppity—and I said, 'Listen, kiddo, you don't have to marry me. I can go to Cuba and have it tended to. You owe me nothing. I never want you to marry me because I'm pregnant.'" She wanted him to be sure this time. (At twenty he had married his childhood sweetheart, Evelyn Franklin. After seven years together, they were divorced in 1949. She later married and divorced Richard Avedon.)

"Of course, I'm going to marry you. You know we're engaged," Milton told her. "I want to marry you and I want to have children."

While Amy organized a September wedding, Milton went off to Hollywood on assignment for *Look*. In their tireless attempt to overtake *Life*, *Look*'s reigning couple, Gardner and Fleur Cowles, had lured him away from Luce's breadwinner with such perks as a $100,000-a-year non-exclusive contract. No other photographer even dreamed of such a deal in 1953. After signing the contract, his first big assignment was a Hollywood story, featuring, among others, Frank Sinatra, Gene Kelly, and the screen's latest blonde bombshell, Marilyn Monroe.

# THE IMAGE MAKER

Milton and Marilyn described their first meeting to Edward R. Murrow on *Person to Person* early in 1955. Aware of Milton's reputation, she had agreed to a sitting despite her bandaged leg. She turned an ankle and tore some ligaments while on location for *River of No Return,* and Joe DiMaggio, her current beau, had bundled her back to Hollywood. She met Milton on the Twentieth Century-Fox lot, expecting something like the Abraham Lincoln of photography. "Why, you're just a boy," she told him.

"You're just a girl," he replied. She giggled, he smiled that smile. Over the next few days he posed her in an opulent setting caressing a balalaika, suggesting languor with a mink stole and nudity under a long black sweater he had borrowed from Amy. Out in Laurel Canyon he had her nestle in the crotch of a gnarled old tree and perch at the base of a scabrous cliff. There was nothing vulgar about the pictures. ("Milton never had to show nudity or sex," says Jesse Rand. "You just knew it was there when he got finished with the job.") When Marilyn was stripping to put on Amy's sweater, Milton said, "Wait a minute," and turned his

back. "I don't mind," she told him. "I do," Milton replied. That kind of respect was new to her. It bowled her over. The pictures reflect it. They brought out an extraordinary depth, a vulnerability.

"She had gone through all the photographers who did the crappy pinuppy stuff," says John Springer. "That is what she did, so she did it, but Milton made her do more. He photographed her as if she were Garbo and she understood this and this was the affirmation she needed."

When Milton sent her a couple of rejects from the sitting, she responded with two dozen red roses and called to say they were the most beautiful pictures she had ever seen. "Whatever she saw in Milton's pictures, she wanted to be that," said Jule Styne, the composer of *Gentlemen Prefer Blondes* who convinced Fox to cast Marilyn instead of Betty Grable in the film version of his musical. "He captured everything that Marilyn was on film. I used to watch him shoot. It was one, two, three, and he had it. He knew that image. It's like a painter, like he created that image." A collaboration had begun.

Although they had not met, Marilyn called Amy a few days before the wedding to congratulate her. "You're so lucky to have a man like Milton love you and marry you," she said, sounding very wistful.

"I know that," Amy replied, "but he's also lucky to have me." Marilyn started to giggle.

"I've never heard anybody say that," she said.

She would call every couple of days, just keeping in touch. "She was obviously fascinated with Milton's lifestyle and very interested in me," Amy recalls. "I was not the least bit interested in her, by the way. To me, she meant nothing at that point."

After their marriage, the newlyweds took a working honeymoon. They stopped in New Orleans, where Joshua Logan was directing Charles Boyer and Mary Martin in the pre-Broadway tryout of *Kind Sir.* Milton received the key to the city—thanks to the play's publicist—while shooting the director and his stars at work. Logan's patience and creativity impressed him.

They moved on to Los Angeles in October to shoot a feature on California fashion for *Look.* He called Marilyn immediately, they got together and talked. She wanted to meet his bride. He said he would arrange it.

Marilyn, here with *Look* editor-in-chief Fleur Cowles, appeared for her first sitting with Milton with a bandaged ankle.

Movie people were not seen on the streets of Beverly Hills on Saturday nights. Nobody went to Romanoff's or Chasen's. They all went to somebody's house or had people to theirs. For a certain group, the creative people from MGM or anybody who was in town from New York, the place to be was Gene Kelly's house. Betty Comden and Adolph Green, Sidney Chaplin, Kay Thompson, Stanley Donen, Roger Edens, among others, would gather there at about six for a big buffet. By eight o'clock they were deep into charades. Gene loved competition and loved to win. He always wanted Amy on his team. She was very fast and always got the answer.

Milton dropped Amy off at Kelly's at six, then went to have dinner with Marilyn. He had arranged for the

The portrait with a balalaika was made at the first sitting for *Look* in September 1953 as was the small
portrait opposite left, showing Marilyn in a makeshift nightgown with a mink stole.

During their first meeting Milton caught Marilyn among the trees in Laurel Canyon, 1953.

women to meet that evening, but decided to bring Marilyn along later. Having heard in the trade about Kelly's gatherings, she was a bit nervous about going. Marilyn really had very little social life at that point. She ate, slept and worked. She was having love affairs, but she did not socialize. They used to call her the mystery woman. "I didn't go out because I couldn't do polite conversation," she told Amy. "I couldn't make table talk, small talk, so I said, 'What the hell, I'll just stay home.'"

Marilyn had no ear for chit-chat or gossip, which is another thing she and Milton had in common. They thought it was a waste of time. "If you can't say something nice about someone," she would murmur, "don't say anything."

"It's only gossip, for god's sake," countered Amy, who liked to know who was doing what to whom.

"I don't know any, because I don't get out," Marilyn told her.

"Don't you talk to the hairdressers on the set, the wardrobe people?"

"I don't pay any attention. It goes in one ear and out the other."

Charades was in full swing when Milton arrived with Marilyn, whose current film, *Gentlemen Prefer Blondes*, was smashing box-office records. "She came in wearing a camel's hair coat over her usual black leotards and a big beige sweater," recalls Amy. "She had no makeup on, her hair was nonplus and she looked like a wet chicken." Everyone greeted them and asked them to join in, but they demurred. Milton was very shy and not quick, so he could not play charades. He tried a few times, but it was beyond him. The two of them sat in a corner and watched the others make damn fools of themselves, yelling, jumping, carrying on. They were mesmerized, like spectators being entertained at a performance.

After a while, Amy went over, plopped herself down and started talking to Marilyn, who was also painfully shy. "Everybody thinks that she was the glamorous Miss Monroe," says Amy. "She couldn't talk her way out of a paper bag. It was almost like Sid Caesar. They both needed to become a character in order to function. She had no social graces whatsoever. She was smart enough to know that this was something missing in her life, which is one of the reasons she left Los Angeles and came to New York."

"You are so clever to be able to do all that," she told Amy at Kelly's. "I wish I could do it."

"You can," Amy decided characteristically. "Just dive in, for heaven's sake. It's no big deal. So you make a mistake." But she never once played charades in the years spent with the Greenes. She was always entertained by it, she just would not try it.

During the Greenes' month-long stay in Los Angeles, Milton photographed Marilyn again. That is when it happened, with the pictures. "What attracted Marilyn to Milton in the first place was meeting him through his still pictures of her," observes the usually reticent Jay Kanter. "I don't know, she seemed to come alive. You could tell that something special was happening. Milton had that quality, too, with other people, but there was a kind of magic between them, something that you could tell was clicking. I mean there was an incredible response from her. It was fun to watch."

This time he had her languishing under clinging sheets, chatting on the telephone in peddle-pushers, lounging in exotic settings with hairdresser Sidney Guilaroff's three pekineses and his discobolus, and Joseph Schenck's suit of armour. The pictures at the Schenck mansion transpired after Milton asked to meet the legendary producer, a founder of Twentieth Century-Fox, who had been Marilyn's mentor and lover—hardly the request of a current lover. "The two of them were just giggly," Jesse Rand remembers when Milton brought Marilyn to his birthday party. "It was almost like a sister and brother between them. I don't know if there was a romance there. I don't know who pursued it if there was."

What there was, more to the point, was a deep mutual respect. And respect seems to be what Marilyn most needed. "She was a great gal," said Whitey Snyder, her friend and makeup man for ten years, "but she had the greatest inferiority complex of any person I've ever known." Somehow, Milton's gentle, deep-eyed understanding assuaged it.

"She wanted something more than love," observes Susan Strasberg, who as a young actress met Marilyn in 1954. "She wanted to be respected. I think she'd come to terms with the fact that maybe everybody wouldn't love her, but she wanted to be recognized for who she felt she was."

Marilyn began confiding in Milton. She shared her frustrations about the brutal way the studio exploited her. "They treat me like a thing," she told him. "I hate being treated like a thing."

"She was just their nutsy little blonde that they would fix up the visiting bigwigs with and all that stuff," Springer explains. "Literally that's how they treated her. She would go out with a guy from Des Moines if she was told to do it. She thought she had to. She was so used to being treated like a studio slut that she didn't realize for a long time how important she was. The studio treated her like shit and then someone like Milton Greene comes along and takes her seriously. He treats her like someone very special and gifted and like an actress, like a person instead of a thing."

She was "the nation's number one sex thrill," according to John Crosby's *Herald Tribune* column, and Twentieth Century-Fox pushed her from picture to picture to capitalize on it. This was the last stand of the all-powerful studio system, the end of the so-called Golden Age of Hollywood, as anti-trust actions divorced studios from their theaters and television changed the habits of moviegoers. Fox, like every major studio in the early fifties, was still a dream factory with twenty-nine producers and an endless contract list. Every month on a Monday a studio talent scout would bring in a bus load of twenty or thirty girls for the producers to evaluate. The lucky ones joined the already bulging roster of contract players. "They were slave contracts," says producer David Brown, who then ran Fox's story department. "Many women were mistreated, if they weren't really tough like Bette Davis was. And Marilyn was no exception. She came out of a very, very humble background. She befriended or was befriended by older men, sometimes studio heads. And unquestionably she performed for them sexually. And the result was a certain loss of self-esteem, a feeling of being victimized, and always the desire to please in order to advance a career which I'm not convinced she was so fervently interested in. But she had to survive."

After *River of No Return,* Fox planned to co-star her with Frank Sinatra in *Pink Tights,* a reworking of an old Betty Grable musical with a new score by Sammy Cahn and Jule Styne. She liked the idea of working with Sinatra, although it irked her that he would be getting $5,000 a week, while her renegotiated slave contract gave her only $1,500. One of the world's top box-office stars, she still received the pay and treatment of any contract player. "I know Sinatra's flying every weekend, from Thursday on, to Spain to see Ava Gardner," related Styne. "He was smitten and trying to make it work. So we'd lie and say, 'Oh, I think he just stepped out.' I knew Sinatra wasn't going to do *Pink Tights* and Marilyn knew, she later told me, she wasn't going to do it. They wanted to work together, but it was a terrible script."

When Marilyn refused the project, they put her on suspension without pay. After years of non-stop picturemaking, it was a relief. She finally married the persistent Joltin' Joe DiMaggio on January 14, 1954. They flew to Japan on a honeymoon trip where the Yankee legend held baseball clinics and his wife unintentionally upstaged him. Leaving Joe to his constituency, she gratefully accepted an invitation to entertain U.S. troops in Korea. The tour made daily headlines, as GI's rioted and behaved like

bobbysoxers. "Joe, you never heard such cheering," she told her husband.

"Yes, I have," he replied, but she never really understood the adulation he had known during his glory days at Yankee Stadium.

She compromised with Fox, agreeing to do *There's No Business Like Show Business*, its latest homage to Irving Berlin, in lieu of *Pink Tights*—with the stipulation that *The Seven-Year Itch* and a $100,000 bonus would follow.

Milton came back in May. He photographed her on a Sunday on the deserted Fox backlot. They ransacked the wardrobe department, which was nothing new to

In October 1953 Milton photographed Marilyn with a pekinese at the home of movie mogul Joe Schenck.

Preceding double page: Milton captured Marilyn languishing under a bedsheet at Schenck's villa.

her. She got most of her personal wardrobe from there, anyway. This time they found the costume Jennifer Jones had worn in *Song of Bernadette*, and he shot her as a wistful peasant on the French village set from *What Price Glory?* They began outlining some fanciful possibilities for their professional futures— nothing concrete, just possibilities.

On September 9, she flew without Joe to New York for location filming on *The Seven-Year Itch*. The next day she reported to Milton's Lexington Avenue studio. With the festive participation of Dom Pérignon, he shot her in various buoyant juxtapositions to a wicker chair, but the highlights of that sitting resulted from a mistake. He captured her as a ballerina—which certainly she was not—when the costume he ordered proved to be too small. "That's all right," he said, "just hold it up against you." Some of the most poignant photographs of Marilyn Monroe emerged, to be sure, but something more. The pictures become generic

portraits of a dancer to challenge even the sketches of Degas.

Joe joined her later that week at the St. Regis. "The phone rings in Connecticut one Sunday morning and this voice says, 'Hello, this is Joe DiMaggio,'" Amy recalls. "I went crazy. This was my god on the other end of the telephone. I grew up at Yankee Stadium with my old man—fifty-cent doubleheaders on Sundays in the sunny bleachers. He was inviting us to come in that night and have dinner with him and

Marilyn. I was beside myself, walking on air. I didn't give a shit about Marilyn—this was Joe DiMaggio."

The Greenes, dressed to kill, picked up the DiMaggios in front of the St. Regis. They drove to the old El Morocco, where they were ushered into the private backroom. Joe would never sit in the front with everybody looking at him. They had a wonderful time, because Milton and Marilyn discussed what had become business as usual, her troubles with Fox, and Joe and Amy talked baseball. Every now and then Milton and Marilyn would look over in astonishment as this elfin creature and "The Big Guy" sat head to head reenacting his great moments against the Red Sox in 1949.

They met again a few days later when Marilyn shot what would become one of the most publicized scenes in film history—her skirt blowing up as she stood on the subway grating. Dozens of photog-

**One of Milton's most famous Monroe sessions was inspired by an ill-fitting white dress with a crinoline. This enchanting series of photos was taken at the studio on Lexington Avenue, New York, in September 1954.**

**Left and preceding double page: Marilyn posing with hairdresser Sidney Guilaroff's statue of the discus thrower. The intensity of her embrace seems to breathe life into the ancient figure.**

raphers and reporters gathered for the big event. Amy was standing with Milton and Joe as, perfectly timed by Billy Wilder, the skirt billowed up, exposing the Monroe anatomy. Milton and every other photographer started clicking away. "And, let me tell you," Amy reports, "Joe DiMaggio was not a happy camper. I saw his face; he became like a crazy Italian. He was seething."

"It's in the film," she said, trying to pacify him. "It's not going to matter." He stormed away.

The foursome dined together again soon after that. The Greenes went to pick them up, but Marilyn as usual was not ready. The men settled in the sitting room. Amy called into the bedroom, "Do you need any help, so we can get moving here?" "Yeah, come on back," Marilyn answered. She had a big old mink coat flung on the bed. "Oh, I'm going to try this on," Amy said. "I've never had a mink coat on before." It fit like a tent, the old Hollywood, dolman-sleeve type, everything huge, down to the floor. "This isn't doing anything for me."

Marilyn giggled and said, "Go on out and tell Milton to get you a mink coat."

So Amy went out and told him: "Milton, Marilyn says for you to get me a mink coat."

"Uh-huh," Milton replied and then laughed. He had no intention of getting his wife a mink coat.

When Amy returned to the bedroom, Marilyn was in a terry cloth robe. She always wore terry cloth. "She takes it off and her body is bruised," Amy discloses. "I said, 'What's that?' She looked at me and I looked at her and she didn't say anything. Instinctively I said, 'Joe.' She said, 'Yes.'" Nothing more was said. Marilyn dressed and they all went to dinner.

Later, Marilyn told her about the honeymoon flight with Joe: "She got up to go to the john or get a glass of water or something. When she came back she spontaneously threw her arms around him from behind. He took her hand and flung it so hard into the air that it broke her thumb. (Now you must realize the size of Joe's hands. He used to take both of mine in one of his like a muff.) He just didn't want to be caressed in public. He wasn't demonstrative at all, yet she told me he was the greatest sexual partner she ever had. In bed he was fantastic."

When Marilyn lived with the Greenes in 1955, she often shared intimacies with Kitty Owens, their cook, housekeeper and resident mother figure. "I kinda liked Joe DiMaggio and I really wanted to get her talkin' 'bout him," Kitty related. "I used to tell her he was a great ballplayer, but she'd never get into the relationship with me. She jes' said, 'Great ballplayers and great husbands are two different things.' That's all she ever said."

# DAVID & THE PHILISTINES

While the DiMaggio marriage faltered—it lasted only nine months—the Monroe-Greene collaboration flourished. Not the sittings. They became perfunctory and mostly documentary for the time being. Marilyn and Milton had bigger fish to fry. From their months of brainstorming, the idea of Marilyn Monroe Productions had evolved, a creative collaboration that would give them control of Marilyn's future projects.

Why had she entrusted her career to a magazine photographer with no track record in the movie business? Yes, he gave her respect and affirmation. Yes, his pictures of her plumbed the depths. But this was the most profitable commodity of a powerful fiefdom run by Darryl F. Zanuck, one of the biggest bastards in a Monument Valley of bastards. Why this David to fight these Philistines? Judy Balaban Quine, a child of that world and a key player in the MMP saga, explained that Milton's camera communicated with and let us communicate with the whole Marilyn, which was an incredible validation for her, because people like Zanuck saw only the most obvious external, blatant representation of her and defined her as that alone:

You know how as a child, if you have loving reinforcement from parents or teachers or friends you see yourself in their eyes and it helps develop the sense that you can handle problems and all kinds of things? I don't think Marilyn got it from anyplace. So the voices that defined her were very rejecting, very critical and very demeaning, and basically that was her sense of self. She was just so wounded that vulnerability is not even the right word. Yeah, there was vulnerability in her, but it was a seriously wounded vulnerability that couldn't find it's way out of that damaged inside. Suddenly, along comes Milton who validates the innocence with the camera and wants to protect that definition. He not only redefines her for herself but he is willing to fight for her redefinition to survive in her career. That's heavy stuff. That's superseductive emotionally for somebody who was so fragile, for someone so wounded.

By the end of 1954, Milton had taken the legal steps required to create Marilyn Monroe Productions. He flew to Los Angeles with the documents to share with his partner. She reacted with pride and awe when she saw papers designating her as president, but it would be her vice president who waged the battle. These were courageous steps indeed at a time when the paranoid studios decried independents of any kind. And he had taken them virtually alone with his New York lawyers Frank Delaney and Irving Stein. "Milton had set up the company before MCA became involved," states Jay Kanter, "and as to ownership of the company, who did what and so on, that predated our involvement."

Girding for the inevitable battle with Twentieth Century-Fox, Milton drafted Lew Wasserman, the president, and Kanter, the New York representative, of the potent MCA talent agency. Potent they would have to be to deal with Fox chairman Darryl F. Zanuck. "He was a tank assault with everything, with everyone, with business, with family," says Quine. "He was kind of a monster person with about as much sensitivity as my brick fireplace."

To him Marilyn was studio chattel, a sexpot that wiggled her ass. It amazed him when the box-office receipts came in, but he would never credit her. It was always Merman's singing, Donald O'Connor's dancing, Jane Russell's tits. It was never Marilyn. "He wouldn't believe she could sing," said Styne. "If you're pretty you can't sing. If you're that pretty, you're not talented, you're a bimbo. Zanuck was a great movie producer, but he had no class."

What he had was power, more power than Vice President Greene could have imagined as battlelines were drawn. After Milton brought in the big guns, it went from a mom-and-pop candy store to corporate war, with daily phone calls, meetings, threats: "He said this ... You said that ... We do this ... We want that ..." It would continue for more than a year.

"Milton's mind worked in devious and strange ways," according to Amy. "He thought he was a good businessman and he really wasn't. He was an artist."

"Oh, God, Milton, take the pictures and leave the business to me," Irving Stein pleaded. "Please do me the favor, don't come to the meeting. Let me handle

it." But this was the most exciting moment of his life. He couldn't let go.

"Now, this poor boy from Brooklyn is touched and blessed by God, anointed, as it were, and he's going to make movies," continues Amy. "This is millions of Saturday afternoons looking up at Fred Astaire and Cary Grant and all of a sudden he's calling his gods, the people he emulates, his friends. So he has all the candy, and she is exhilarated by all this, so I, as a young bride, I'm going along. I think it's terrific because I see him walking on air. Am I going to be the one to stick the pin in the balloon? I'm too smart for that."

Marilyn flew East incognito for Christmas with the Greenes. She was, in fact, escaping from Hollywood and Twentieth Century-Fox, with a baffled press in frenzied pursuit. "That put us all into a little cadre of sort of road-company secret service agents," recalls Quine, "because the whole thing was so hush-hush— where she was, how she was." Aware of Milton's involvement, the press staked out his Lexington Avenue studio, his pied-à-terre on Sutton Place South and the Weston house on Fanton Hill Road. The Greenes outmaneuvered them by meeting Marilyn's flight and heading straight for Connecticut. They stopped outside the village of Weston, deposited their precious cargo in the trunk and smuggled her past the paparazzi crowding their driveway.

Marilyn would spend a good part of the next two years in Milton's self-styled paradise, attached, as was her wont, to yet another surrogate family. "All of a sudden, she moved in with us, moving vans and everything, and from there we lived like one family," remembered Clyde Owens, Kitty's husband, who looked after the Connecticut place. "She was very pleasant. She liked the kids and we all would have our little cookouts and things like that. That was during the time he had got her away from that group, from Twentieth Century-Fox, because I used to get the calls from Darryl Zanuck. He was calling there all the time. But to us she didn't show any strain of business, anything like that. She was just like us, a regular person in the house."

Any strain was absorbed by her business partner, who had mortgaged his house and borrowed from friends and associates to finance MMP. But he was confident and she was happier than she had ever been. "The two of them knew a secret," says Amy. "I lived with it every day, but I didn't know the secret. When they planned and schemed they would be on the sofa and I would be in a chair next to them and they went right off into their own world that only the two of them understood. He would start to say something and she would say, 'Gee, I was just thinking of that,' and vice versa."

Marilyn stayed in a guest bedroom, all purple like a little tent, with a nice bathroom where she liked to take bubblebaths. Amy poured in all the stuff for her the afternoon after she arrived, and went to answer the phone. When she came back the room was all steamy and the bubbles were everywhere. Marilyn was sitting in the tub, her blonde hair done up with a top knot, her skin rosy with no makeup whatsoever: "I looked at her and said, 'You know, you're really very pretty.' It was the first time the tough LA bimboess left her and she became strawberries and peaches and cream. She looked up, smiled very sweetly, and said, 'Thank you.' It was a nice moment."

"When I first met her, she was so pretty," said Kitty. "She was a beautiful person, kind and sweet and generous, very considerate. She considered you, you know." She would come into the kitchen ready to help. Kitty was dubious, but Marilyn would snap the stringbeans for her, break them up, and say, "Is this the right size?" Kitty would tell her, "Jes' snap 'em, they ain't got to be even." Marilyn would do a lot of things, even peel potatoes, but she left the mashing to Kitty: "I'm going to let you make me creamed potatoes. Nobody makes them like you."

One day Kitty found her scraping spinach off the high ceiling of the rustic kitchen. "Kitty," she confessed timidly, "I had a little accident." She had opened the pressure-cooker too soon and the green stuff went ballistic.

"She could be real funny at times," Kitty recalled with a deep smile. "Oh, we had some good laughs together."

Amy had a portrait of Abraham Lincoln that Marilyn loved. "He's my hero," she told Kitty.

"He's lots of people's hero."

"I know, but he was such a great guy. When I see a man like that, I would love to just sit on his lap."

"I can't imagine seein' you settin' on ole Abe's lap," said Kitty and they laughed and laughed at the thought.

When Gene Kelly came to visit one weekend, they all went water-skiing off Milton's boat. Milton insisted that Marilyn wear a life jacket—he was not about to let the biggest asset of this fledgling company drown in Long Island Sound. So there she was, wearing what is called for obvious reasons a "Mae West," totally top heavy and trying to get up on water skis. Suddenly Kelly placed a hand under each buttock and with a satisfied, "Ahhh!" pushed her up until she stood. Milton took off and she squealed with the delight of waterskiing for the first time.

Everybody came to the Greenes on weekends. They never sat around a table with less than eight or ten people. It was a continuous hotel. Josh and Nedda Logan, their neighbor Audrey Wood, the literary agent, Leonard and Felicia Bernstein, Richard and Dorothy Rodgers, Mike Todd sat around telling theater stories. Marilyn would sit mesmerized with eyes as big as a cat's drinking in all this wonder. Sometimes she would say to Amy, "Do you mind if I don't come out tonight?" She closed her door and nobody bothered her. "We had our own life," Amy emphasizes. "We were not living through her. She was living through us, goddamn it. Nobody seems to understand this."

When Joyce and Bob Saffir, old friends of the Greenes, drove out for the weekend, Joyce asked,

1

2

3

6

**1** Milton bonded with his sons during their deep-sea fishing excursions.
**2** Milton and Amy pose with little Joshua on a porch glider.

**3** Clyde Owens shot the Greenes in Weston. Amy holds Anthony; Milton holds Joshua.
**4** In front of the Beverly Hills house they shared: Milton shot Marilyn, wearing the camel's hair-cashmere coat he and Amy had given her.
**5** The houseguest tends Joshua while Amy and her friends, George and Marisa Nardielle, face Milton's lens.
**6** Marilyn stands proudly with Amy,

Paula Strasberg, and Joshua beside her new Cadillac at Twentieth Century-Fox.
**7** The star plays with Joshua outside her *Bus Stop* dressing room.
**8** Marilyn and Kitty Owens examine their booty on Christmas morning in Weston.
**9** Marilyn and stylist at a *Look* sitting in Los Angeles, 1953.
**10** Amy took this father-and-son portrait.

"Where's Marilyn?" She wanted to meet this celebrated creature.

"Oh, she's very nervous about new people," Amy told her. "She's shy and afraid to come out. She's been in the bathtub for an hour." It amazed Joyce that this famous woman would be afraid to meet her.

"So finally she did come out," Joyce relates. "She didn't wear any makeup, I remember. She was scrubbed clean. She was just beautiful in pants and a sweater. She sort of sat off in a corner and didn't speak." The others went about their business, gossiping, laughing, catching up. "She would go off by herself and sit on the stairs, kicking her leg, just sitting there. I thought, frankly, there was really something wrong with her. I started thinking she was out of it."

They all sat at the kitchen table for dinner, the soup, the food, and still she did not say much. They sat around the television to watch Walter Winchell. He mentioned her name and someone said, "Marilyn, he's talking about you," and she went, "Oh-oh." Then Bob Saffir, a wonderful storyteller, started recounting his war experiences, and that got her. She finally broke down and started laughing and enjoying herself.

When some late guests arrived, they started playing charades. Milton and Marilyn left. "I saw the two of them in another room," says Joyce. "And the way they were, if I were Amy, in love with her husband, I wouldn't have liked it." But Amy understood.

Marilyn loved walking in the woods. This troubled Kitty, who feared some fanatic might stalk or harm her. But nothing scared Marilyn. "Oh, there's nothing out there," she would say, and go off for her daily constitutional, sometimes taking the Greenes' baby along. She loved little Joshua, who was almost a year old. She would snuggle him on her bed in her terry cloth robe, piling pillows around him and ruffling his hair. She used to babysit on Kitty's night out.

Not only did she want three or four children of her own, she told Kitty, but she would adopt children of all nationalities. It distressed her when someone warned against adopting Indian children because they were particularly difficult. "No, they ain't," Kitty protested. "If you give 'em love and affection they're jes' like any other kid."

Kitty remembers Marilyn's accounts of growing up in foster homes: "One lady that she spoke of was very nice, but some of 'em wasn't too good to her. And that used to bother her. She said if she ever had children she would treat 'em nice and if she adopted a child she'd be real sweet to it."

"People don't realize how they hurt a child when they don't give it attention and just have it work and yell at it," Marilyn told her. "I think a mother should take a child sometimes and just say, 'I love you,' put her arms around it and hug it."

"She used to tell me how her mother was sick, and that used to touch my heart," Kitty said. "I think if her mother had been well and had raised her that would have been so nice. But sometimes things like that are just not, you know, not meant to be."

Kitty tried to put a bright face on it: "Well, look how lucky you are, Marilyn. You got to be a star."

"Yeah, Kitty, but there are other things in life, too, that you need while you're getting to be a star. And if you don't get them, you'll miss them."

She confided her greatest fear to Kitty: "She thought that maybe she might become mentally ill when she got older."

"What?" Kitty snapped. "How can you sit there and say that?"

"Well, it might run in my family."

"That has nothin' to do with you. You don't let that happen to you." As one of the ten depression-era children of a Virginia sharecropper, Kitty knew a thing or two about indomitability.

"You can inherit that," Marilyn insisted.

"Well, you can, but you don't have to inherit that. If you sit there and keep harpin' on it you'll make yourself sick."

Around the time that Marilyn came East, Judy and Jay Kanter had their first child. Marilyn came by to see her at feeding time, so Judy said, "Come on in with me." She hesitated, feeling, somehow, that this was a sacred place and she was an interloper. "No, no," Judy urged. "Come on in." She sat on a day bed absolutely awestruck as Judy fed the baby her bottle. "Would you like to hold her?" Judy asked. Stark terror crossed Marilyn's face. "Come on, sit here, it's so easy. Don't worry about it. You won't drop her." She sat frozen on the day bed. "Don't you want to?"

"It isn't that," she said. "If I hold her maybe she will be like I am."

Judy already had talked enough with her to know

At the press reception announcing the formation of Marilyn Monroe Productions in 1955, the president played the role of CEO magnificently.

that she identified with her mentally ill mother: "In essence she was saying, 'If I hold your baby she will also be insane.' Later when she got pregnant, I seriously doubted she'd ever achieve the harmony to carry a child to term. I wish I wasn't so sure of it. It's heartbreaking."

Milton continued to bait the Philistines with renewed confidence. His lawyers had found tunnel-sized loopholes in Marilyn's Fox contract, so on January 7, they held a press conference at Frank Delaney's townhouse to announce the formation of Marilyn Monroe Productions. Among the celebrities on Milton's guest list was another Hollywood sex goddess from a bygone era. "I looked down and there coming up the stairs was Dietrich in black with a veil," recalls Joyce Saffir. "I didn't want to stare, but I did stare: Marlene Dietrich, come on! She looked around, and it wasn't very long, maybe ten minutes, fifteen, then she went down the stairs and out. Milton greeted her, Marilyn came over, but it wasn't her show."

It wasn't anybody's show but the president of MMP's. Milton, decreeing white for the occasion, bought her a white mink—not ermine as some claim—coat. The rest was left to Amy. She went to Norman Norell, who said, "Dress her very simply, no ruffles, no frills, no glitz." They decided on a short, white satin dress with thin straps. Marilyn wanted it tighter across the buttocks. Norell said, "No." She wanted it tighter across the bust. Norell said, "No." For the first time she was not poured into a dress. Amy found matching satin shoes and even white stockings. None of the regular manufacturers made white hose then, so she went to a nurse's uniform store. Her only jewelry, a pair of dangling diamond earrings Amy borrowed for the evening from Van Cleef & Arpels, were the first real diamonds she had ever worn. She looked brilliant, absolutely dazzling, and the press attacked like ants to sugar. As hard as Milton tried to keep things dignified, the paparazzi invaded and all hell broke loose.

When the furor somewhat abated, guests descended upon Marilyn and the Greenes with dinner plans. "Amy?" Marilyn asked. "What would you like to do?"

"I'd like to see Sinatra at the Copa, but we'll be here so bloody long, we'll never get in."

"You want to see Frank Sinatra?" Marilyn said. "Come on. Just the three of us. Don't invite anyone else."

They entered the Copacabana on street level and walked around the bar. The minute they got past the first bouncers, one of them ran ahead, saying, "Marilyn Monroe is here!" They went downstairs to the nightclub and Marilyn stood there at the entrance, a shimmering vision in white. The place was packed. There was no room to breathe. Sinatra was singing, but dozens of people, headwaiters, goombah bouncers, started milling around Marilyn, and no one paid any attention to him.

"Hold it," he snapped at the orchestra. "What's going on here?" She didn't move. She just stood there shimmering with Amy and Milton huddled behind her. People started whispering, "It's Marilyn Monroe. It's Marilyn Monroe." Sinatra was not happy. All he wanted was to get the show over with and leave.

"Get her a table and chair, for Chrissakes," he ordered, "And let me get on with the business at hand." Out of nowhere a table and three chairs appeared. They were seated directly in front of Sinatra. Marilyn slithered out of the white mink coat and the place went wild.

"When the show's over, Sinatra tells Milton to come upstairs and we'd go out to dinner," Amy relates. "He never speaks to Marilyn, but directly to Milton. It's so Italian. You know, you don't talk to the broad, you talk to the guy."

They got up to leave. The entire audience was waiting to see this woman, touch this woman, be near this woman. People began crowding in, pulling at Amy, ripping her skirt, trying to get to Marilyn. Amy became claustrophobic as fists and elbows grazed her head

and body. "Milton, they're going to kill me," she kept repeating.

Suddenly Marilyn grabbed her and started giving hushed orders: "Put Amy in the middle and do what I do. Don't panic, if they see you panic you're finished. Just smile. I'll get you through this." With Milton in back and Amy sandwiched in the middle, Marilyn led the way, taking mincing little steps, smiling at everyone, saying "Hi, how are you? Nice to see you … " It was like the parting of the Red Sea. She got them out.

"Never again," Amy vowed up in Sinatra's dressing room. "I'll never be seen with you."

"I got you out, didn't I?"

"Yes, but you also almost got me killed." (Amy later devised a disguise for her—brown Prince Valiant wig, maternity outfit, low-heeled shoes—which allowed her to go about unrecognized. Marilyn did not like it. "She liked to work the crowds," Amy says. "She liked to be recognized. She liked to have the power to part the Red Sea.")

The four of them went to 21 after Sinatra's show. Marilyn and Frank were adorable together. They liked each other. "Rumor had it that they were lovers before, during and after," Amy discloses, "but Frank always backed off because he respected Joe DiMaggio. Once Joe left the scene, Frank stepped right in. Was Marilyn promiscuous? For that point in time you bet she was, but not in a whorey way. Marilyn was in love with love. She was always searching for it and she wound up ruined because she always fell in love with the wrong man. She was the type of woman that's always looking for that exhilaration, that headiness of love, but won't wash a guy's socks out, you know, the practicality of love, the building of a love she couldn't handle."

The official announcement of MMP galvanized Twentieth Century-Fox. Zanuck, who had recently

**Two legends met when Marilyn posed with Marlene Dietrich at Marilyn Monroe Productions' press party.**

jumped from head of production to chairman of the company he founded, remained obstinate. "Let her go," he railed. "I don't want her around here. 'Strawhead'"—his derogatory name for her—"isn't blackmailing my studio." The money men in New York disagreed: "You can't let her go; she's bringing in more money than anybody." Zanuck finally relented so far as the fine legal points were concerned, but he stopped short of giving "Strawhead" creative control. "The money he would have given in a minute because he knew he could make it back," Amy maintains. "What he couldn't stomach was giving what he considered a blonde bimbo choice of directors and scripts." Besides his personal bias, he knew that capitulation would set a dangerous precedent for the all-powerful studio system. The battle raged on, with Milton remaining loyal to his partner in the face of great temptation. "You've got to be a poker player," Jesse Rand told him. "You got Marilyn. Zanuck wants Marilyn. Make peace with the man. Say, 'Here's what I want: I want to be a producer.' They'll open up Milton Greene Productions for you on the lot. It's stockholder's money, man. It's done every day: 'Here's a three-picture deal; take a backseat on Marilyn.' All they want to do is get pictures from her and all you want to do is make pictures." Good, pragmatic advice, but missing one incalculable factor: The irrevocable bond between the partners of MMP.

"No, no," Milton insisted. "Now we've got him where we want him."

"I don't think Milton really knew how powerful these men were," Rand says. "You could win a battle, but you never won the war. I never knew anybody who could blackmail a studio." When Buddy Adler, a reasonable man who replaced Zanuck as head of production, did offer Milton a three-picture deal without Marilyn, he refused.

On the heels of the MMP announcement Milton and Marilyn agreed to appear on *Person to Person*, Edward R. Murrow's popular television program. They told Amy that they only accepted because of her mad crush on Murrow. Actually, they saw it as a chance to promote MMP on national television and give Fox a tweak. It worked. Even before the telecast Zanuck started calling CBS with threats of legal action, which MMP's lawyers quickly dispelled. Preparations proceeded. Since the Greenes' house sat in a valley, adjustments were necessary to facilitate Murrow's televised visit. Two weeks before the scheduled telecast, a CBS crew descended on Weston to build a 150-foot tower on the lawn. Chaos ensued, but not to the exclusion of supplementary activities.

Mike Todd, whom Milton adored, came out for a weekend during one of his frequent broke periods. He was producing a benefit for the Arthritis and Rheumatism Foundation—"half to charity; half to Mike," claims Amy. He was assembling celebrities to augment the opening night of Ringling Brothers' circus at Madison Square Garden. "I really want to use Marilyn," he said, "but what am I going to do with her?"

"Put her on a pink elephant," Milton suggested without missing a beat. He must have pulled it from the subtext. Todd cheered. Marilyn giggled. And so it came to pass.

The grand old hulk on Eighth Avenue nearly burst with eighteen thousand spectators applauding celebrity guests and circus acts. Backstage, pandemonium reigned as Milton in his dinner jacket adjusted Marilyn's glittering costume and supervised the painting of the elephant in time for the grand finale. "They were painting this elephant pink," recalls Jay Kanter, "working until the last minute to get it done, still touching it up and trying to hoist Marilyn on top at the same time." Then, suddenly it just happened.

"And now, Ladies and Gentlemen," announced Milton Berle, the guest ringmaster, "you will see a vision on top of a pink elephant."

Those big old doors opened and there stood that shocking pink elephant with Marilyn, all spangles and

Marilyn astride a pink-painted elephant created pandemonium at Madison Square Garden during the charity circus in 1955.

feathers and bosoms, perched on top. "The place went absolutely ape," says Amy. "I have never experienced anything like the hysteria and the din that came out of those mouths all the way up the stands. I'm telling you, I had goosebumps."

Amy shared a box with a sophisticated crew that evening. Milton Berle's caustic wife, Ruth, the Art Buchwalds, the Robert E. Sherwoods stood cheering and clapping as Marilyn passed and acknowledged them with a sweep of her arms. "She's the most sensual, exciting woman I've ever seen," remarked Sherwood, one of America's foremost playwrights.

Milton and Jay stood like statues on either side of the big doors, waiting for the elephant to make the circle of the old Garden. Then the trainer prodded the creature and its radiant cargo into the center ring, and it was bedlam, absolute bedlam. "It was at that instant

that I realized her power, because up to this point I hadn't understood," Amy admits. "She became Marilyn Monroe, whatever Marilyn Monroe was."

Edward R. Murrow mentioned the Madison Square triumph during the *Person to Person* program on Good Friday. "It meant a lot to me, because I'd never been to the circus as a kid," Marilyn told him, securing with millions of viewers her Little Match Girl image. Otherwise, she seemed subdued to the point of torpor ("That's not an actress," I remember my father saying during the telecast in 1955. "Barbara Stanwyck's an actress.") Milton was virtually tongue-tied. Although they did manage to plant the MMP mine, Amy stole the show. She kept a lively exchange going with Murrow and told about the time she was taking Marilyn back to the St. Regis. "Hey, you know who's in there?" the taxi driver asked, turning excitedly toward

7

8

9

10

1 Milton shot Marilyn and Milton Berle, the ringmaster, costumed for the Madison Square charity gala, 1955.
2 Milton arranged for Marilyn to appear at Milton Berle's Friars' Club Roast.
3 *Look* editors, Jack Hamilton and Fleur Cowles, chat with Marilyn about her first sitting with Milton.
4 *Look* editors pose with Marilyn after the first sitting.
5 Milton looks on proudly as Joshua gives Marilyn a drink.
6 Milton records Whitey Snyder preparing "The Showgirl" for a scene.

7 The star sits with one of her crew at the *Bus Stop* wrap party.
8 The embattled couples: Vivien Leigh/Laurence Olivier and Marilyn Monroe/Arthur Miller hold a press conference at Heathrow Airport in 1955, after filming *The Prince and the Showgirl*.
9 Marilyn relaxes at 480 Lexington Avenue, Milton's penthouse studio.
10 This costume worn for publicity shots was later replaced for the Madison Square event.
11 Milton Berle welcomes Marilyn to his "Roast" in New York, 1955.

11

the two women. "No, who is it?" Amy asked. "Marilyn Monroe," he told them.

The day after the telecast, Milton got a call from Jean Negulesco, the director, offering Amy the lead in *Bonjour Tristesse.* Marilyn was not pleased; Milton was adamant: "No, she's a housewife."

"Just a minute," Amy snapped. "Don't make those kinds of decisions for me. Let me think about it."

"You're right," he said. "You have two hours." She thought about it and decided against doing it. Several months later she met Negulesco. "You were perfect," he exclaimed. "I knew it, you were perfect." Eventually Otto Preminger directed the film with Jean Seberg in the role.

Soon after Marilyn settled in Connecticut, Amy made a suggestion to Milton: "This is a very dull life for her. She's never really lived in New York. Get her an apartment in New York and let her spend a couple of days a week there. She can always come back to us." It was not merely altruism on Amy's part. She needed her own privacy, as well.

"When you are servicing that kind of an account, it's exhausting," Judy Quine maintains. "You get caught up in the sheer business nature of it, the personal needs and the burden of that kind of trust, and everything else goes by the wayside. Amy got rather impatient about having plans disrupted at the last minute because something came up with Marilyn—something always came up with Marilyn. Amy would be bugged, but it was never about him off boffing Marilyn and she was jealous or anything like that. It's just that after awhile enough is enough. You want a little bit of your own life and time and space."

The first place Milton found for her, a suite at the old Gladstone Hotel on East Fifty-second Street between Lexington and Park, was straight out of Edith Wharton, all red velvet and very plush. Marilyn giggled at that plushy place, and took it like a good sport. "When I'd leave her," Amy recalls, "I'd look back and she seemed very small and wanted to be brave, but

she really was intimidated by all that Victorian grandeur."

Since the Gladstone was right around the corner from Milton's studio, they managed their first formal sitting since Marilyn's arrival in New York. He shot her in the opulent white mink, in a cuddly terry cloth robe, and straddling a studio stool. You can tell they were preoccupied.

The actress Leonora Corbett told Amy at a dinner party that she wanted a three-month sublet for her Waldorf Tower apartment. Amy looked at it the next day and took it on the spot. On a high floor with light pouring in, bright and fluffy in blue and gold and a bit of white, it delighted Marilyn. She perked up and began her New York life.

That life included strains that would enrich and confuse the radiant waif from Hollywood. She studied at the Actors Studio, that spawning ground of The Method, where Lee Strasberg held court as guru and Svengali. Strasberg, a founder of the politicized, depression-bred Group Theater, and his actress wife, Paula, latched on to Marilyn and she, in turn, became dependent upon them. Some say they made an actress of her. Others, like director Elia Kazan, say she became their "perfect victim-devotee."

Amy, never hampered by understatement, puts it this way:

> Nobody was using Marilyn. Paula was a slob, but that was Paula. I never took Paula seriously and I never

A very private Marilyn at breakfast in her hotel suite in New York, September 1954.

Following spread:
While on location in New York for *The Seven-Year Itch,* Marilyn frolics in Milton's studio wearing one of the terry-cloth robes she liked so much (page 50).
Milton, silhouetted with pipe, looks on as Bauman and Marilyn play photographer and model (page 51). Photographer unknown.
Milton's former partner, Marty Bauman (right), kibitzes as Milton sets up a shot (page 52). Photographer unknown.
The striking result is on the following page (page 53).

took Lee seriously, not for one moment. In the discussions I would have with Paula, she was a total airhead. A woman who couldn't talk about anything of importance. She didn't have an artistic hair on her head. She was a frustrated actress. She was a frustrated mother. She was a frustrated everything. This was an unhappy lady. And Lee was so dour and morose that after half an hour with him you were ready to jump out the window. These were not my two favorite people. I got along well with their daughter, Susan. She at least was smart, charming and fun. The Strasbergs were not a day at the beach, but Marilyn was fascinated by them. I personally didn't care one way or another. It annoyed Milton because he thought he saw that they were diminishing him in her eyes, but they didn't really.

Nevertheless, in November, Amy sponsored a benefit premiere of *The Rose Tattoo* film, which raised almost $100,000 for the financially stressed Actors Studio. Marilyn and Marlon Brando, who served as ushers for the event, reported to Milton's studio for some playful publicity pictures. It was Brando who had first recommended the Actors Studio to Marilyn, and who, according to Amy, was "having a little thing on the side with her."

Marilyn's big thing at the time was Arthur Miller, whom she had met in Hollywood three years before. The celebrated author of *Death of a Salesman* was then experiencing a lull in his career and, as a target of the anti-Red witch hunt, turmoil in his life. The mutual attraction that emerged may well, on her part, have been intensified by her penchant for underdogs. A romance flared almost immediately, and coupled with Strasberg's belief in the kinship of analysis and acting, led to another of her dualistic encounters. "She started with a psychiatrist because she had a big guilt thing about being a homewrecker," says Amy. "When she started seriously with Arthur, who was still married, she felt deeply embarrassed that she was still being called a homewrecker. You must understand, at this point in her life the only thing she wanted to do was

make classy movies and become a class act. She wanted to be a lady more than anything else in the world."

Milton brought her to Dr. Margaret Hohenberg, a Vienna-trained Hungarian, who had previously psychoanalyzed him. Contrary to some reports, Milton and Marilyn were not treated concurrently by Dr. Hohenberg. Milton had graduated before Amy met him. He loved to tell how all of a sudden on the couch one day he started singing Irving Berlin's "I don't need analyzing/It is not so surprising/That I feel very strange but nice … " He jumped up and said, "Dr. Hohenberg, it has been terrific, but I think I'm going to leave you."

For Marilyn it would be a different story. Led to the analyst's couch by her affair with Miller and her flirtation with The Method, she would grow dependent on psychoanalysis. For the rest of her life she went three or more times a week, often opening doors that might better have been left closed.

By the winter of 1955, the partners had decided on their first two projects. Audrey Wood, their next-door neighbor in Connecticut, called Milton: "I have a young client, William Inge, who's written a play called *Bus Stop* I want you to read. I think it's a perfect film vehicle for your partner." Audrey would never mention "Marilyn" on the telephone, because she always feared "the enemy" had bugged it. They read the play, then went to see it when it opened on Broadway a month or so later with Kim Stanley in the lead. They knew that Cherie, the broken-down "chantoosie," was the role to introduce the new Marilyn Monroe.

The second vehicle started as a William Wyler project. He wanted to film Terence Rattigan's play, *The Sleeping Prince* with Marilyn and the play's original star, Laurence Olivier. Wyler called Rattigan in England and offered him an all-expenses-paid trip to Hollywood to discuss it. When he reached New York, on the first leg of his journey, a message was delivered to him at the airport: Marilyn Monroe wanted him to join her for

Marlon and Marilyn, who were having a brief fling at the time, clown around
for Milton's camera to help raise money for the Actors Studio.

cocktails in the Barberry Room at 4:30 that afternoon.

She swept in an hour late wearing dark glasses and
followed by Milton, Jay Kanter, and Irving Stein.
Marilyn, who seemed to be in control of the meeting,
presented her case in such a quiet, shy way that the
playwright only understood about every third word.
He got the gist of it, however: If Wyler did not make
a definite offer she would buy the rights. She talked in
hundreds of thousands of dollars, rather than tens of
thousands as Wyler had. When Rattigan agreed, she
took off her sunglasses and gazed at him with knowing
innocence: "Do you think there's a chance that Sir
Larry would do it with me?"

Rattigan met with Wyler in Hollywood, but his
producers made no firm offer. On his way back

through New York, he telephoned Marilyn and told
her the rights to *The Sleeping Prince* were hers.

With Fox still holding out, MMP was low on cash by
the end of 1955. Milton and the company suffered a
great loss when Frank Delaney left their employ. The
man who had brilliantly spearheaded the legal battle
against Fox felt he could no longer endure what he
perceived as Marilyn's lost confidence in him. That this
could be a forecast of things to come completely
escaped Milton. "I found Marilyn at times to be
unreasonable," says Jay Kanter, "but I think that was
largely brought about by her being very suspicious of
people's motives as to wanting things from her. She
had a deep fear of people wanting to use her and a
kind of wall went up. As much as you'd try to say,

1

4

2

5

3

6

8

7

9

10

1 Milton prepares Marilyn for her spectacular entrance at Madison Square Garden in 1955. (Photographer unknown.)

2+3 At the old Ambassador Hotel, Milton and Marilyn discuss their *Person to Person* appearance with Edward R. Murrow. (Photographer unknown.)

4 Milton and Marilyn arrive in Los Angeles to film *Bus Stop*. (Photographer unknown.)

5 The photographer and his favorite subject evaluate prints in the New York studio.

6 Milton managed this self-portrait during his first 1953 sitting with Marilyn.

7 Amy shot her husband and his partner cavorting in Richard Rodgers' Connecticut swimming pool in June 1956.

8 An unknown photographer captured Milton and Marilyn at an early *Look* sitting.

9 Milton and Marilyn chat with Maurice Chevalier before a session at the New York studio, 1955. (Photographer unknown.)

10 Milton poses at 480 Lexington Avenue, his penthouse studio, with Marilyn and Sammy Davis Jr. before shooting the singer's first album cover in 1954. (Photographer unknown.)

'Marilyn, it's all for you, that's what we're doing if for,' she wouldn't buy it."

The Greenes moved Marilyn into their apartment at 2 Sutton Place South and moved themselves over to Milton's studio for their nights in town. Marilyn liked the bright little one-bedroom pied-à-terre, where she could meet Arthur and entertain friends. Kitty and Clyde Owens remembered the Christmas Eve party she gave there.

By that time the Owenses were on the MMP payroll. "Milton put us on that payroll, took us off his books and put us on that," said Clyde. "That was his shrewdness." Kitty cooked for Marilyn. Clyde drove for her. They both helped out when she entertained, which was usually on the spur of the moment. She called Amy in Weston on the day of her Christmas Eve party for some extra plates. "What are you serving?" Amy asked. Marilyn did not have a clue. Kitty cooked up a vat of beef stew for her and she and Clyde drove into New York with it.

They brought the plates and the food into the kitchen and started changing into their work clothes. "What are you doing?" Marilyn asked.

"Well, I'm settin' up," Clyde said.

"You and Kitty go right in there and sit down," she told him. "Fix yourselves a drink and join the party." She had about twenty guests and a guitarist named Clarence Copeland playing and singing. Arthur Miller was there. Kitty did not take to him: "I had a sixth sense about him that he wasn't a hundred percent sincere. It just dawned on me. And maybe I should

have said it. She was really fascinated by him. She knew he was real smart, but I jes' didn't think he had Marilyn at heart."

On the way home that night she shared her feelings with her husband: "I hope she don't marry him, Clyde, because he'll jes' use her. He thinks he's too wise. If he marries her I think he's gonna destroy her."

"That's their business," Clyde said. "As long as they're happy … "

Such dire premonitions were far from the minds of the principal players on New Year's Eve, 1955. On that day the clouds rolled by, the sun came out, the bluebird of happiness warbled its tune. In other words, Twentieth Century-Fox finally capitulated. Marilyn would make four pictures for Fox over seven years, but she was free also to make pictures independently with others. She would have complete creative control over her projects. She would be paid the long overdue $100,000 bonus for *The Seven-Year Itch* and receive $100,000 per picture plus a weekly $500 for personal expenses during filming. Yearly, through MMP, Fox would pay an additional $100,000 to her and $75,000 to Milton. Also, the studio would pick up MMP's option on *Bus Stop* and buy it as her first picture under the new contract.

The victors gathered at 2 Sutton Place South— Marilyn, Amy and Milton, Judy and Jay. Marilyn's favorite Dom Pérignon flowed freely as they jumped up and down, crying, "We beat them! We beat them! We beat them!" They couldn't stop laughing, giggling. The future was theirs.

# THE FRUITS OF BATTLE

Nineteen fifty-six got off like a cannon blast as the principals of MMP prepared to decamp for Hollywood. Their New York pace quickened while the Fox deal was finalized and Milton sustained some last-minute reversals. Although it had been agreed that he would control MMP with fifty-one percent, Marilyn, or her advisors, who increased daily, suddenly demanded the controlling interest. The vice president relented, accepting forty-nine percent of the company he created.

Milton discovered also the hazards of negotiating with a major studio. "Dealing with those guys up there, you're in their ballpark," says Jesse Rand. "It's the oldest line in Hollywood, you know, 'Trust me' in producer talk means get fucked." Despite the fact that Milton functioned as *Bus Stop*'s producer, Buddy Adler would receive the screen credit. In fact, Milton Greene received no credit whatsoever on the picture he, more than anyone, nurtured. There was one consolation. Adler, a decent and intelligent man, turned out to be a godsend. Throughout production he ran interference between MMP and the studio, where, according to Michael Korda, "everyone from Zanuck on down wanted him to fail just to teach Marilyn a lesson."

Still, the exhilaration of participation and the relief of finally striking a deal seemed to assuage Milton. After all, while playing in their ballpark, he had won a big game. "He loved playing the mogul, that goddamned big thing with all those Hollywood people," attests Joe Eula. "He loved the fact that he could throw around names like Metro and Fox the way you talk to your maid about getting the windows done. It was just mad. But Marilyn needed a daddy, somebody as strong as he who gave the impression of being an intelligent businessman. Well, his intelligence in that regard, as far as I'm concerned, was always negligible, and now that he's dead, he has no way of being able to say, 'Watch it!'"

With the financial burden lifted after over a year, Milton moved Marilyn over to 444 Sutton Place so that he and Amy could retrieve their pied-à-terre. In order to support himself, his family, Marilyn and MMP, he had maintained his lucrative photography business, while negotiating with Fox, planning *Bus Stop* and squiring Amy and Marilyn around town. He would sleep three hours, get up and start working at the crack of dawn. If they had slept at the studio after a night on the town, he would wake Amy and send her with a coat thrown over her pajamas to the Kanters' apartment. While Jay prepared for work in the bathroom, she would hop into the still-warm bed next to Judy for a few more hours of sleep.

At the end of January, Milton and Marilyn had their first relaxed sitting in ten months. They worked for the only time in Connecticut, shooting her as a fresh and wholesome country girl in a tennis sweater, another bright red one, and by an old railroad trestle near the house.

The following week back at the studio, they shared what is probably their most celebrated session. The so-called Black Sitting not only yielded some of the most enduring images of Marilyn Monroe but served as a dry-run for the visualization of Cherie in *Bus Stop*. Joe Eula sat in on the shoot as it became progressively more relaxed with the consumption of champagne and caviar. "The clothes go off and the goddamned hat goes on and the pictures are always just perfect and they were never vulgar," Eula observes. "They aren't glamorous pictures, in fact they border on being funny, on being a joke, comedic with fishnet stockings and a black hat and black this and that and a glass balanced on her knee and a big rip going up the ass, but they are gorgeous. They have that wonderful little-girl attitude, having a good time playing dress-up."

Milton had that extraordinary faculty of being able to direct his subjects into those revealing attitudes. That was his genius. He never used his "rubber lens" in a vulgar way, but always in the most attractive way to extract an essence. He made them feel that they were not giving their all but getting it. "You're going to get what you give," he implied, and, therefore, they would give it all.

During this hectic period Marilyn lunched with John Springer, who had left Fox for the public relations firm that handled MMP. Madness and pandemonium hit the streets as people began to recognize and follow her until they reached the safety of Gallagher's. Once inside, she was among peers. Myrna Loy and Henry Fonda, both friends and clients of Springer, happened to be lunching at separate tables. They both came over, partially to see Springer, but mainly to meet this fabulous Monroe. Loy, warm and gracious, behaved as if she were so honored to meet Marilyn. Fonda was charmed. Marilyn was just paralysed. "Myrna and then Hank Fonda, and to Marilyn they were the real thing," says Springer. "She was like a child, these were movie stars. She wasn't a star. She thought of herself as some kind of pretty freak that people chased and screamed at."

Chance meetings at Gallagher's had nothing on her next celebrity introduction. "We were like two little fourth graders meeting their hero," Judy Quine says of herself and Marilyn at the prospect of meeting Sir Laurence Olivier. The actor-knight arrived in New York during the first week of February to publicize the premiere of *Richard III* on NBC. RCA had purchased the rights to his monumental film as a big promotion for color television, and for the first time a major theatrical film would be introduced on the small screen. During his visit he planned to meet with Marilyn and Milton to finalize their co-starring venture in *The Sleeping Prince*. Terence Rattigan, also in town for the meeting, would adapt his play, while Olivier had been lured into the project with the promise of directing and co-producing as well as co-starring.

They set the meeting at Olivier's hotel on the day of the telecast, a very rainy Sunday in New York. When Jay Kanter, who represented Olivier and Rattigan in America, arrived, Olivier offered gallantly, "It's such a bad day, we can't make her come here. We'll go to see her." So they all headed over to Sutton Place, where Milton greeted them at the door. "And we're all waiting for Marilyn, who was in the bedroom just too frightened to come out," recalls Kanter. "We waited, and we waited, and we waited. We waited a couple of hours. I'll never forget how embarrassing the whole thing was. Finally, with Milton's persuasion, she did come out, and Larry and Terence made her feel so comfortable."

In that particular case, the conflict which prompted Marilyn's pathological lateness can be readily explained. "Pre-Milton, pre-star Marilyn is in worshipful awe of this actor and feels unworthy to be in the same room with him," relates Quine, "but the new Marilyn is going to talk about co-producing a movie in which they co-star and she wants him to like her and respect her talent. So which Marilyn do you get to be?" She stayed in that bedroom for two hours because the new Marilyn was working to make the old Marilyn worthy of going out and meeting Sir Laurence Olivier as an equal or co-star or human being.

When she did finally appear that day, Olivier later claimed, she had been so adorable, witty, and physically attractive they were at her feet in a second. Considering his reverence for punctuality, it is curious that he failed to see the incident as a harbinger of conflict to come. Indeed, congeniality prevailed when they reported to Milton's studio two days later for publicity pictures. Sitting side by side, Olivier right, Rattigan left, Marilyn in between, they bantered, bussed, and generally made merry for Milton's camera.

At noon, they repaired to the Terrace Room of the Plaza, where Milton had set up a press conference. During the announcement of the forthcoming venture, Rattigan was somewhat bemused by Marilyn's repeated assertions that she and she alone "owned" his play. But the best was yet to come. As the proceedings continued, a strap of Marilyn's already revealing dress popped, causing media mania. Whether or not she had prearranged the "accident" is a moot point. "That famous, supposedly set-up scene, where the strap broke, it wasn't set up," insists Eula. "It

broke." Olivier, well aware of having been upstaged, was not displeased. He needed a commercial hit at this point in his career, which he felt "was in a rut." As a hundred and fifty reporters and photographers closed in, he realized that their project would be properly launched. "Olivier knew what he was doing," continues Eula. "He knew what he was getting into. She was the biggest thing going."

The following week, Marilyn nervously made her first live stage appearance in an Actors Studio workshop performance. You couldn't get into the Studio that day. Everyone was there, Marlon Brando, Montgomery Clift, Kim Stanley, to watch her perform part of the barroom scene from *Anna Christie* with Maureen Stapleton. She scored as Eugene O'Neill's downtrodden heroine. "It was a great performance," recalls Springer. "She was so exciting. It was suddenly seeing a great actress doing a great, difficult role, and she was more human than Garbo." Strong praise, indeed, for a twenty-minute acting-school exercise, but an indication that Marilyn and The Method were compatible. The Strasbergs used it to advantage. Playing on her insecurities, convincing her she could never do *Bus Stop* without Studio input, Lee demanded $1500 a week for Paula as Marilyn's acting coach. Milton chafed. Marilyn insisted. Buddy Adler said, "Pay her!" to keep the peace. So Paula Strasberg, during the filming of *Bus Stop,* received more than most of the production's essential contributors, the same salary Marilyn had been getting under her old Fox contract. "When we was in California, Paula was always with her, supposedly helpin' her," said Kitty Owens. "Bad medicine, that one. I didn't care too much for her, but I shouldn't say that. My mother always told me not to say bad 'bout nobody."

On February 25, the East Coast menage transplanted itself to North Beverly Glen Boulevard in the Westwood section of Los Angeles: Milton and Amy with two-year-old Joshua; Marilyn and her personal maid, Florence; Kitty and Clyde Owens; and

David Maysles, Milton's assistant, who later became a noted documentary filmmaker. The spacious nine-room furnished rental, designed with suites and servant's quarters, made a decidedly communal arrangement tenable.

"That was kinda hectic and pretty good, too," said Kitty. "It was nice. My job mostly was workin' with the Greenes, but Marilyn used to like for me to cook for her." She favored vegetables, which Kitty cooked to her taste: stewed tomatoes, stewed corn, fresh string beans, red cabbage with apples and squash of every kind and shape. "She loved chili and her favorite was scramble' eggs with rolled anchovies and capers, but those things they didn't want her eatin', you know, 'cuz they wanted to keep her figure. Mr. Greene would say, 'You gotta be thin, thin, thin!' So if Mrs. Greene caught her eatin' fatty food, she'd grab the plate off the table, sayin' 'You's on a diet, Marilyn. You's too fat now!'"

Marilyn had her own peculiar vanities, as well. One of Clyde's jobs was bringing bags of ice upstairs every morning to fill a big basin for her. She would stand on that pile of ice until it melted. "Marilyn, you gonna get sick," Kitty warned.

"But, Kitty," Marilyn explained, "if I do it every day it will make my legs firm." One day she came down with a bad cold.

"Honey," Kitty told her, "it's from standin' on that ice."

They were there to make a picture. The household revolved around it. "I went because my husband was at work, but Los Angeles isn't my favorite place in the world," Amy admits. "I made as much of an adjustment as I could, but I was very lonely."

Milton and Marilyn got up at six. The car picked them up at seven. That is, it arrived at seven. "She'd keep 'em waiting sometimes, about forty-five minutes, if not more," recalled Clyde. "I don't think a whole lotta times she was sure whether she was in control of herself or not. I think she had that feeling. Florence used to kinda rush her to get dressed to be ready for the limousine, but Marilyn would always have to see that her bras and everything fitted. She didn't just run out looking any kinda way."

They worked all day. They got home late after viewing the rushes, Kitty gave them a lean dinner—besides keeping Marilyn on a strict diet, Milton was always dieting himself—and Amy would read lines with her to prepare for the next day's scenes. Everybody was in bed by eleven to start the cycle all over again the next morning.

Milton's celebrated "eye" worked overtime on *Bus Stop*. From the moment he saw the play, he had visualized Cherie's physical characteristics. "Now, wait a second," he told Marilyn and Amy during intermission. "This is a woman who never sees the sun. She sleeps all day, so forget Max Factor's Pancake Number 22. It's too perfect. She's got to be white, white all over." He spent hours working with Whitey Snyder, her makeup man, and her hairdressers to develop the look of Cherie. Before she faced the cameras, he would actually pat her with baby powder to whiten her hands, arms and shoulders. The first day of shooting, when she came on the set in costume, he looked at her, made her turn around, walked over and snagged one of her fishnet stockings. "What are you doing?" she fumed. "Now I'll have to change."

"Just relax. You're a tootsie from Miami Beach, a 'chantoosie.' You're going to have holes in your tights."

Milton chose Joshua Logan to direct *Bus Stop*. Although primarily a theater person, he had just completed the successful film version of *Picnic,* another Inge play. Milton knew him as a fine actor's director, one who would protect Marilyn and pamper her when necessary. "Josh adored her," says Amy. "He would no more raise his voice to Marilyn than kick her." Also, unlike most Hollywood directors, having studied with Stanislavsky at the Moscow Art Theater, he countenanced The Method. Not only would he tolerate Marilyn's academic soul searching but, as a friend of Lee Strasberg, he could handle Paula.

"Paula used to drive directors wild," says John Springer. "Not only with Marilyn but with her daughter, Susan, before her. When Susan started doing a few movies, Paula drove everybody crazy, because she directed her. Sidney Lumet and others tried, but it was Paula who told Susan just what to do and how to do it, and she did the same with Marilyn, as much as she could get away with." Logan endured it and quietly superseded her coaching in order to appease the star. In fact, Logan seems to have been almost Chamberlainian in the business of appeasement.

"Whenever Marilyn and I got alone together, Josh would be behind the set listening to our conversation," recalls Don Murray, who became her leading man. "He was very eager for us to get along, and if there was any kind of argument going to start he wanted to be there to jump in and stop it."

Milton originally wanted Rock Hudson to play the amorous cowboy opposite Marilyn, but the actor kept vacillating. Marilyn, at Milton's urging, even telephoned Hudson directly: "Why aren't you doing this? I really want you to work with me. I think the two of us would be absolutely sensational together. Please think about it?" Without explanation, he turned her down.

Fifteen years later, Amy, as a Condé Nast editor, conceived the first movie issue of *Glamour*. She brought Roddy McDowall to the Brussels location of *Darling Lili* to photograph Rock Hudson. One evening, as the three of them dined and shared movie lore, Amy said to Hudson, "I have to ask you a personal question. Why did you refuse to do *Bus Stop*? It would have been perfect for you."

"I know," he agreed. "When I saw it, I realized I'd made a terrible mistake."

"Was it because of Marilyn?"

"It had nothing to do with Marilyn. When Milton photographed me for American Airlines, he didn't treat me well, so I didn't want to work with him."

"But Milton's the sweetest man in the world," McDowall interjected.

"I could kill you," Amy snapped. "A grown man can't pick up the phone and say, 'You did this, this and that, let's talk about it'?"

"You're right," Hudson conceded, "but I couldn't do it." And that was all he would say about it.

Determined to find out what happened on that

Marilyn embraces her *Bus Stop* leading man Don Murray at the start of shooting, although it wasn't always "Hearts and Flowers" between them.

American Airlines shoot, Amy investigated. "A proposition was made," she discovered. "Milton refused and forgot about it, but Rock was too embarrassed to work with him again. For that he gave up *Bus Stop*. You want to talk about meshuga?"

Josh Logan had someone else on tap. A young actor named Don Murray had impressed him playing small roles on Broadway in *The Rose Tattoo* and *The Skin of Our Teeth*. Between those two shows, he had spent nearly three years as a social worker in refugee camps throughout Europe.

It was something of a culture shock for the twenty-six-year-old actor, going from thirty dollars a month as a social worker to fifteen hundred a week as a Hollywood actor, from refugee camps to the Fox lot. His stint in Europe had coincided with Marilyn's rise to fame. He had seen *Gentlemen Prefer Blondes* in Italy dubbed in Italian, so he had never even heard her voice. He had no idea of the magnitude of her stardom when he reported for rehearsals. Marilyn behaved very simply, like any other working actress. She read her lines so softly he had trouble hearing her, but she seemed dedicated to her craft. "I didn't see the whole stardom thing," Murray recalls. "I hadn't been exposed to that yet, so I thought, 'This is a very, very serious actress.'"

Actual filming began on location in Phoenix, Arizona. The night before shooting the first scenes, they had a read-through in Marilyn's hotel room. All fresh and scrubbed, she greeted Murray in one of her terry cloth bathrobes: "I looked and said, 'My God, she has skin like a baby's, she hasn't a line on her face.' She had one of the most beautiful skins I've ever seen. She just looked like a child, absolutely exquisite without any makeup on."

The next day all hell broke loose. Murray and the production were hit by a media blitz. The newcomer had to elbow his way through dozens of cameras and newspaper people just to get on the set for the rodeo sequences. The relaxed Marilyn of the rehearsal period disappeared. "She became very nervous about working," Murray continues. "I think that's why she was always late. She would get there on time, but then she would fuss over makeup and wardrobe. She just wanted to avoid getting on the set as long as possible. But let me say, according to people who had worked with Marilyn, *Bus Stop* was her best-behaved movie. They say she was more nearly on time than for any other picture, that psychologically it seemed to be a terrific period in her life. She had Milton with her, who was very helpful. She had Josh, who was gently persuasive. She had

Paula Strasberg coaching her, which was a comfort to her."

For someone coming from the stage discipline it was a unique experience, but Murray adapted to it. Other stage-trained actors were not so flexible. The memory still rankles Eileen Heckart forty years later. "It was the worst professional experience of my life," declares the usually congenial actress. "It was so terrible, I don't want to talk about it."

"The working conditions?"

"Yeah, the whole situation; I don't want to tell you why."

Murray tries to put it in perspective: "The only thing I can think of is that Eileen was referring to the same things that we were all affected by, but that it affected her more deeply than it did Hope Lange, Arthur O'Connell, or myself. Besides the fact of working in a goldfish bowl, and Marilyn being late, even though less late than on her other films, Marilyn had a very short attention span. When you did a scene with her, she would be excellent for a couple of lines and then lose character, so that you'd cut and have to start again."

That created difficulties, particularly for stage actors accustomed to performing without interruption. Whenever they did a scene with the star it would be stop and go, and since her performance was put together in little bits, her best takes would be used. It almost didn't matter what others did. They had to try to be at their best with every scene, every take, every line, every word every time, because no matter how bad they felt about it, that piece could be the one used if it was good for Marilyn. Realizing those were the rules of the game, Murray adjusted. Perhaps Heckart, with far more stage experience, found such flexibility understandably more difficult.

"See, there's a certain group of actresses, and Heckart must be one of them, that believes the theater and the acting thing are sacred," Jule Styne reasoned. "Marilyn doesn't know about that. She says, 'It's a place where I'm invited to come in, but only

because I'm sexy.' I can't accurately quote her, but it's that insecurity. She never outlived that."

Another disturbing element of working with a superstar was the reactions of those around her. Nervous assistant directors, production assistants, and the like created an air of anxiety on the set. How does Marilyn look today? How does Marilyn feel today? They were so worried about the star they ignored the needs, the reasonable desires of others.

Don Murray, for one, had more than reasonable needs. He reached Phoenix with a hundred-and-three temperature, the result of a bout with pleurisy. He admitted himself to hospitals there and later in Sun Valley every weekend, so huge needles could be plunged into his lung cavity to extract fluid. He would return by seven Monday morning to the set, where the studio had not even provided a cot, let alone a trailer for him. As leading man with extremely physical business to perform, he had no place to rest between scenes until he found an old table to stretch out on. Murray came to expect such indifference from studio personnel with one notable exception: "Milton was never that way. He was always very warm and very considerate to me. He knew this was my first film and he was as helpful as anyone could be while still taking care of his major responsibility. I have a great opinion of Milton."

Murray remembers Milton being very much present, seeing to everything so that Marilyn could concentrate on creating the role. The press was always milling around, but he kept them from interfering, particularly when she consulted with Paula about her performance. He seemed to respect, if not Paula's ability, Marilyn's belief in it. Meanwhile, he shot production stills and the costume portraits of Marilyn for the film's

Between shots of *Bus Stop*'s rodeo sequence Milton captured this unusual pose.

Following spread: Marilyn rehearses her "Old Black Magic" number with choreographer Jack Cole's assistants.

provocative advertising campaign. (During one of these on-set sessions, Marilyn fell off a step, landed on the floor unhurt and told Milton to keep shooting. That incident was exaggerated, allegedly by *Bus Stop* screenwriter George Axelrod, into a fall from a six-foot ramp, after which Milton callously continued to photograph his prize property while she writhed in pain. Well, dear reader, you decide.) In addition to his other responsibilities, Milton would be consulting constantly with Logan and with Milton Krasner, the cinematographer, about lighting and the look of the film. Much of its visual texture and the rich detail of the star's performance resulted from her partner's flawless "eye." One small example of his uncredited contribution is in her "Old Black Magic" number. That inspired business of kicking the spotlights on as she sings and gyrates was conceived by Milton.

While the company moved from sultry Phoenix to Sun Valley, Idaho, for wintry exteriors, the powers that were viewed the rushes at Fox. "We like them," Logan was told. "There are just two things. Number one, Monroe's makeup is too white. We're going to have to reshoot some closeups of her because it's just too pasty. She looks like a clown. Our stars have to be beautiful. Number two, Murray's performance is too big. Maybe you can do that on Broadway, but it doesn't work in the movies, especially not in CinemaScope. They'll be running from the theater when this guy comes on. Get a film actor. Replace him."

"Number one," Logan replied, "the makeup is just right. This is a girl who lives indoors and that's the look we want. Number two, Murray's playing the part exactly as I want. You people play things so close to the vest, you seldom get anything brilliant. I told him to come on like Attila the Hun and that's what I'm getting." Only one executive agreed with him, but fortunately it was Buddy Adler, the head of production. Marilyn stayed white and Murray stayed put.

After a week of filming rugged exteriors high above Sun Valley at the North Fork General Store, the company returned to the studio. Reported bickering between the partners about MMP paying for Lee Strasberg's California visit or the forthcoming presidential elections—Milton favored the urbane Stevenson, Marilyn the paternal Eisenhower—did not diminish the exuberance of their first formal sitting since leaving New York. Again they rifled the Fox wardrobe department and ranged the backlot like giddy children. Employing such enhancements as a black raincoat, a white fox boa, a chinchilla wrap, a hard straw boater and a soft felt homburg, he posed her as everything from a storefront gypsy fortuneteller to a breezy streetwalker. On the way home, he captured her in her Cadillac convertible embracing, in no uncertain terms, a portrait of her idol, Abraham Lincoln.

As filming continued on the soundstage, Marilyn concentrated on using her emotions for the first time to create a character. This impaired, somewhat, the technical necessities of filmmaking. She kept missing her marks, those marks on the floor actors must hit in order to keep in focus and in the proper light. After the first week of filming, Logan approached her leading man: "Don, Marilyn gets excited and misses her marks. If you see a shadow on her face or you happen to notice that she's off her mark, when we're cutting you above the waist just put your hands on her hips and move her onto her marks." So, there was this stage actor doing his first movie, trying to hit his own marks, trying to do an accent and play the emotions of his character, moving this experienced movie star around on the set.

Another of what Murray called his "little prop and costume jobs" required more delicacy. The scene where he storms into her room and wakes her up was complicated by Marilyn's insistence on playing in the nude to feel the character. "Cherie would be naked," she decided, "so I'm going to be naked." As they

Returning from one of her backlot photo sessions, Marilyn posed in her Cadillac convertible with a portrait of her lifelong idol.

played the scene, she kept squirming out of the sheets.

"Don," Logan whispered, "you know when she uncovers herself? Just slip your hand down subtly and cover her up again." As he did so, he noticed that her body was all red.

"It was amazing," Murray says, "because her very smooth baby skin all of a sudden had this rash like hives all over it. And then I realized that it must have come from nerves. I realized how nervous she was about acting, because that's the only time she would get it."

They continued with the scene. "What are you doing in bed?" he asks. "It's almost nine o'clock."

"Nine?" she replies. "I didn't get to bed until five."

"Five o'clock? No wonder you're so white and pale," he is supposed to say. Instead it came out: "No wonder you're so white and scaly."

Everybody started to laugh. "Scaly?" Marilyn repeated. "Ha, ha, scaly." No reference was made to her skin and the scene went on.

Two days later, as they waited to go on the set, she approached him: "Don, you know the other day when you said 'scaly' instead of 'pale'? Well, you know what? That was a Freudian slip."

"Oh, really?"

"Do you know who Freud was?" He nodded. "Well, Freud says that a snake is a phallic symbol and you said 'scaly' which is like a snake which is like a phallic symbol and a phallic symbol means sex, so you were thinking about sex at the time and that's why you said 'scaly'. You know what a phallic symbol is, don't you?"

"Know what it is?" Murray replied. "I've got one." She missed the point.

"Marilyn was a very intelligent person, there's no doubt about it," Murray avers. "But she was a very uneducated person in the sense that whatever education she had came late. She was going through things at the age of thirty, like reading Freud and Stanislavsky, that you did in your teens." He likens conversations with Marilyn, who was four years his senior, to talking with a teenage sister.

"When you looked into Marilyn's eyes, it wasn't like looking into an adult's eyes," confirms Susan Strasberg. "You know, most adults become already closed off or veiled, particularly if you're famous and new people are constantly assaulting you. Marilyn didn't have the defenses that older people have. It was almost like looking back at another adolescent."

That adolescent quality is one of the reasons proximity never aroused her leading man, even when they endlessly reshot love scenes for the censors because she kept opening her mouth while kissing. Aside from the obvious diversion of courting and

marrying nubile Hope Lange during filming, Murray maintains that the aura of tension surrounding Marilyn hardly encouraged voluptuous feelings toward her. He did not think of her as sexy at all. She never aroused sexual feelings in him, nor did she seem to from the other men on the set. "How does she make you feel, honestly?" he would ask the crew. "You're so close to this famous sex symbol, do you get sexually aroused when you see her partially naked in these love scenes?" Not one of them said, "Yeah, I really have a thing for her." Murray discovered that actresses who were not considered sex symbols seemed to arouse the men sexually and romantically much more—Lee Remick and Eva Marie Saint, actresses like that, not Marilyn.

Although rumor circulated that Marilyn resented having a newcomer rather than a major star playing opposite her, only one confrontation marred three months of shooting. During the scene where the cowboy tries to drag Cherie off to his ranch and she finally turns on him, the actress became extravagantly emotional. Screaming, "Leave me alone, you ain't got the manners to give a monkey," she charged him, pummelled him with clenched fists and knocked him out of camera range. The camera stopped and Logan took Murray aside: "Don, I'm getting wonderful emotion from her and I don't want to interfere with that, so stand your ground no matter what happens. Don't let her push you away. Just brace yourself if she does that again." Then he turned to the crew and said, "Nobody cuts until I say, 'cut.' When you think the scene's over we might get something I want to use."

They did it again. She came charging at him, bounced off his chest and fell to the floor. Murray broke character, rushed over to pick her up, saying, "Marilyn, are you all right?" She got up, seemed dazed for a second, then went on with the scene. She repeated her lines, grabbed the sequined tail of her costume he had ripped off and ran out as scripted. Logan called, 'Cut,' and she returned.

"Was that all right?" she asked the director. They were nearing the end of the filming; Logan wanted to get it in the can. He turned to the cameraman:

"Was it all right? Can we use it? Are there bits you can use?"

"I think that was good," Marilyn said. "I think that was a good one." For the first time since the picture began, Murray interfered:

"Wait a minute. It might have been great for Marilyn, but I was afraid she hurt herself and broke character. I picked her up as Don not as Bo. You can't use that for me."

She reacted pettishly: "Oh, my God, can't you ab lib?" Not ad lib but "ab lib." They set up and did another take. She went through it almost as emotionally but better, less over the top, until she grabbed the sequined tail. She paused, stared at him, then slashed it across his face. One of the sequins made a cut under his eye and it started bleeding. Furious, he followed her, intending to give her hell. Logan ran after him, calling, "Where are you going? Where are you going?"

"I'm going to give her a piece of my mind. I'm really pissed."

"No ... no ... no ...," the director muttered and told him about a great Roman general who won all the wars by avoiding the battles. His metaphor so amused Murray that he broke out laughing and dismissed the whole matter. "I've read that we were feuding from day one on that picture," Murray relates. "That's absurd. If I was feuding with a superstar like Marilyn Monroe from day one, I wouldn't have been there on day two."

The day after their bout she sidled up to him and initiated another of the serious conversations she seemed to favor with him. "Do you think a leopard can change its spots?" she wondered.

"You mean if people can change their personalities or their nature?" That was exactly what she meant, and they had a long discussion about whether people can fundamentally change. History was full of examples, he told her, like Saul in the bible, who started by persecuting the Christians and became their greatest leader. She listened with that adolescent intensity, questioning the feasibility of such transformations. In retrospect, Murray realizes she was questioning her ability to adapt to what would be expected of her in a marriage to Arthur Miller: "She was going clandestinely with him then, at least, I didn't know about it and I don't think the public did. Here was someone thought of as a sex symbol with this intellectual who, I guess, wanted a family woman kind of wife. It's crazy that someone like Miller would expect that from someone like Marilyn. Who did he think he was marrying, the girl next door?"

Clandestinely, indeed. Miller had established residency in Nevada in order to obtain a quick divorce, which visits to California could have jeopardized. "On weekends the Greenes went their way, Marilyn went her way. That's the way it was," recalled Clyde Owens. "She'd tell me what time to meet Miller's plane and have me stock the apartment at Chateau Marmont with cheese, champagne, stuff like that." Clyde did not share his wife's premonitions about Miller. "He seemed to be very nice to my way of thinking, but sometimes he seemed to be trying to indicate like he wanted her to break off from Hollywood and New York and establish herself in England, that her being a movie star would be even more appreciated there, greater than it would here. Always he was stressing that point." At the time, with the FBI on his trail trying to uncover proof of Communist affiliations, and a London production of one of his plays as his primary professional prospect, England would certainly have seemed an attractive option.

On May 16, they completed principal shooting on *Bus Stop*. Amy, with Joshua, Kitty and Clyde, drove back to New York. Milton, Marilyn, her maid, Florence, and David Maysles stayed on at North Beverly Glen for retakes and another sitting. He captured her dramatically embracing a statue in Sidney Guilaroff's foyer, but the highlight of the shoot is a prim "graduation picture," taken because she told him she had never had one. They flew back to New York a week later, arriving a day or two after the others.

Nearly forty years later in his Monroe biography Donald Spoto claims that the Greenes stayed on after Marilyn and left the rented house in a shambles. "If you work for Amy Greene, you're not gonna leave a house in no mess," protested Kitty. "I used to tease

her. I said, 'You like those kids, those Gold Dust Twins in the ads, always beatin' dust.' If there's any dust, an ashtray an inch off center that lady sees it. In no way did we leave that house dirty." Spoto uses this "demolition job," as he calls it, to underscore implications of Bacchanalian revels and substance abuse, even quoting Amy Greene out of context to justify them.

"We never had 'wild parties,' we never consumed 'prodigal amounts of alcohol and drugs,' as he puts it," asserts Amy, a teetotaler. "I mean, give me a break. At

that point in their lives those two human beings were so clean, because they loved what they were doing. They would wake up and couldn't wait to get to the studio. It was a happy time. It was the only time Marilyn was out only one week the entire shooting schedule. She was out a week because she was banging Arthur. She said she had a head cold and that she was disappearing and went to the Chateau Marmont. But she had worked so hard so quickly that they were ahead, so Josh shot around her."

Milton and Marilyn both took prescription drugs. He took diet pills and an occasional tranquilizer. She took those and sleeping pills, but Milton certainly did not encourage her intake and they never indulged in so-called recreational drugs together. "He used to try to keep her away from pills and stuff like that," said Kitty. "He didn't want her usin' pills and drinkin'. See, I kep' my ears open and I listened. He didn't want her usin' things like that, and while she was with the Greenes she was clean. But Marilyn was hardheaded, she was wise with people that advised her wrong. She listened to all these people who used her and I don't think that was Mr. Greene. She had him a hundred percent in her corner."

There was a different consciousness toward pacifiers and tranquilizers in the '50s. People did not understand the long-range affects. They were wonder drugs, prescribed miracles. "Marilyn wasn't into drugs," says Eula. "She was a pillpusher, prescription. We were all on those things—blackbirds, upbirds, bluebirds, over-the-rainbow birds. Everybody carried them around in their briefcases like you do aspirin."

In Hollywood, they were already de rigueur. Terence Rattigan described the story conferences he attended at the time: "The first thing they always do is

**While experimenting in Hollywood with costume and make-up ideas for *The Prince and the Showgirl*, Milton shot a pristine "graduation picture" for Marilyn because she said she had never had one.**

hand out tranquilizers—little pills that keep you working and keep your temper. The desks are piled with them—all colors, sizes, shapes. The consumption is fantastic."

Hard drink and drugs never played a large part in the professional and social lives of Milton and Marilyn during their years together. Their objectives and achievements took precedence. "During *Bus Stop* Marilyn was not zonked out at all," Amy confirms. "And the year before that, when she lived with us, she was not zonked out at all. It was what Josh Logan called her 'Golden Period.' So for Mr. Spoto to say that prodigal amounts of alcohol and drugs were consumed is absurd. He's a well of misinformation, gossip and innuendo. How dare he!"

The partners were filming in England when Don Murray and Hope Lange attended a private screening of *Bus Stop*: "We were floored by Marilyn. We couldn't believe how good she was. All of us stage actors, Eileen, Hope, and myself, never believed she was going to be that good because we only saw these tiny pieces and then *stop*. We couldn't envision it cut together. She did wonderful comedy, drama. She was very real. She tore your heart out. It's one of the best performances in the history of talking films."

When the picture opened on August 31, the critics were not far behind Murray with superlatives. Her performance was considered a revelation, the picture a delight. "Then, afterwards, when I was nominated for an Academy Award and she wasn't, I couldn't believe it," continues Murray. "It absolutely astounded me that the industry hadn't recognized how good she was." But in those days, the studios manipulated the Oscars. Without ad campaigns in the trades or mailings to academy members, a nomination was hard to come by. And Fox had other priorities.

When the studio publicity chief told Murray about his nomination for best supporting actor (he lost to Anthony Quinn), he added, "Isn't it amazing?"

"Why?" Murray quipped. "Don't you think I deserved it?"

"Yes, but nobody was pushing for you. We were pushing *Anastasia* and *The King and I.*" For best actress they backed the stars of those films, Ingrid Bergman, who won, and Deborah Kerr, who was nominated, not Marilyn Monroe—a decision made at the top.

Marilyn unjustly blamed her director for the slight, because a particularly dramatic crying scene had been cut from the release print. "You cut my scene," she raged when she saw him again. "You cut my scene."

"I didn't cut it, Marilyn," Logan explained. "The studio cut it."

Susan Strasberg witnessed that exchange. "I always wondered if the studio hadn't cut it in an unconscious way as an act of hostility," she speculated, "because it's the kind of scene that would have gotten her an Academy Award nomination. And she was devastated that she wasn't nominated for that film."

Perhaps Zanuck had the last laugh on his "Strawhead" and her partner, after all.

# THE SPOILS OF WAR

Late on Thursday afternoon, June 28, Milton sent Kitty and Clyde on the tiresome drive from Wilton to Hartford to pick up the results of Marilyn's blood test. The following evening, at the Westchester County Court House, she married Arthur Miller in a quiet civil ceremony without one reporter or photographer catching on.

A traditional Jewish ceremony followed on Sunday with family and friends at the upstate home of Miller's agent, Kay Brown. Marilyn, after six weeks of instruction, had converted to Judaism. "I did the same thing," says Amy. "Elizabeth Taylor, Sammy Davis did it. It was the thing to do in the mid-'50s."

Kitty baked an elaborate cake for the reception without enthusiasm: "All at once I see that she's marryin' this man and it kinda saddened me. It wasn't none of my business who she married, but she was such a sweet little girl and I didn't take kindly to him too much. Like I told Clyde that time, 'I think he might destroy her.' I jes' had that feelin'." Kitty was not the only one, it turned out, to have second thoughts.

Amy and Hedda Rosten, Marilyn's matron of honor,

dressed the bride in a cramped bedroom of Brown's converted farmhouse. (A week before the wedding Marilyn had come to Amy: "You wouldn't mind, would you, you're so secure in your life, if I make Hedda my matron of honor? It would mean so much to her.") Hedda and her husband, the poet Norman Rosten, had reunited Marilyn and Miller in their Brooklyn house the previous year. The poet became Marilyn's cultural guru, while his rather sweet but alcoholic wife became her part-time secretary. "Marilyn was so good hearted she always picked up people that nobody else liked. That was her modus operandi," Amy observes. "She was perverse: If you didn't like that statue, she liked the poor statue because nobody else did. She was really a nice human being."

They arrayed their nervous friend for the occasion in a beige chiffon dress designed by John Moore and Norman Norell, with Amy's own wedding veil dipped in tea to match. Milton supervised as usual, but he seemed worried. Knowing Marilyn as he did, he felt her anxiety. "I haven't seen you smiling all day," he told her. "You sure you want to go through with this? If you don't, just tell me now and we'll quietly go out the backdoor, get in the car and it's over. We'll annul the civil thing."

She looked at Milton with the trust reserved only for him. Her body sort of slumped down, her shoulders relaxed and she said, "What the hell, we invited the people, let's do it." Milton took her out and literally handed her arm to Lee Strasberg, who, appropriately enough as her current father figure, gave the bride away.

Marilyn Monroe and Arthur Miller were married by a rabbi in front of Kay Brown's fireplace. Milton placed the traditional glass under the groom's foot, he shattered it, everybody yelled, "Mazeltov," and hugged and kissed. The twenty-odd guests, Arthur's parents, brother and sister, cousins, Milton's mother, Jay and Judy Kanter, George Axelrod, among them, moved to the flagstone terrace, where long tables had been set for the wedding feast. Milton, always comfortable with camera in hand, was twice blessed. He busily took still pictures and also shot a 16-mm movie of the festivities. Miller seems to be scowling in most of the frames. "Arthur was always scowling," says Amy. "I mean, I don't think he's been happy since the day he was born. And Marilyn was having a good time. If she was gonna do it, by God, she was gonna do it. She was effervescent. She was a bride."

Even before they left for England, the intricacies of MMP's second venture assailed the vice president and duly designated executive producer of the new film. While he, Kanter, and Irving Stein juggled the demands of Warner Brothers, who were financing and distributing the film, with those of Olivier's production company, additional pins complicated the act. First of all, "that slimy Lee Strasberg," as Amy calls him, resorted to blackmail: "If you want this picture to go on, you will pay Paula $2500 a week all expenses paid and she will work with Marilyn, because without Paula, Marilyn won't do this movie." That was more than anyone on the picture but the two stars received. It

was outrageous, but Milton's hands were tied. He knew Marilyn thought she needed Paula. Whenever he brought it up, she would say, "No, no, no, I don't want to talk about it."

Again, Lou Wasserman said, "Pay the bastards!" Now, this was not charged to MMP, but to production cost, which infuriated Olivier, because ultimately it would mean some $40,000 less for him and Marilyn as producers. Marilyn also insisted that Hedda Rosten, at a salary of $200 a week, accompany her to England as personal secretary.

Less specific, but more insidious was Arthur's participation. The bridegroom, asserting his connubial rights, became a long-range hazard. From the beginning of their courtship, with his writing career in low, Miller had half-heartedly overseen MMP business. Even Milton, who had blind faith in his partner, became wary. "Arthur Miller was putting a lotta pressure on the whole business thing," said Clyde, "so Milton came to me and asks me to report on Marilyn's activities from my end of it, which kinda got on my nerves. I sat down and talked to him face to face. I told him that I was on the payroll for both of them, and I thought it was best for me to do my work and keep my mouth shut about either one."

Distracted by the House Un-American Activities Committee and his impending divorce, Arthur had remained a relatively harmless diversion during *Bus Stop*. But the sanctity of marriage and his wife's general insecurity gave him the all-clear to meddle in earnest. Although both Milton and Olivier wanted extensive rewrites on Rattigan's placid script, Miller thought it excellent, thus diluting the impetus for the overhaul it needed. "Milton was an outsider, but because of his visual eyes the movie men respected him," claims Amy. "He thought film. Arthur thought words so he was excluded. Larry could talk to Milton. Jack Cardiff, the cameraman, could talk to Milton. You couldn't do that with Arthur. It wasn't that he was ostracized—he was boring. Who needed him? He was the third wheel. So his only petulant move was to sick the star back at the guys making the film."

The American invasion reached Heathrow in waves during the second two weeks of July: first Milton and Irving Stein, then Marilyn and Arthur, followed by Amy and Joshua, Paula and Hedda. When the Millers arrived, Sir Laurence, his wife Vivien Leigh, and Milton were there to welcome them, along with two hundred avid gentlemen of the press and seventy bobbies to control them. Strained congeniality predominated as the four principals sat awkwardly in an airport reception room fielding questions from the paparazzi. Milton hovered in the background fending off reporters, generally protecting the illustrious quartet. That arrangement—Oliviers and Millers up front, Milton in a subsidiary position—seemed ominous. Five months before, when they returned to Hollywood for *Bus Stop,* it had been Marilyn and Milton fielding questions in the airport lounge.

The executive producer had taken a charming house, Tibbs Farm, across from Ascot racecourse, where he settled in with Amy, Joshua, and an English couple to tend them. Kitty and Clyde had been scheduled to come, but Milton eliminated them when the expense of Marilyn's entourage skyrocketed. Nevertheless, Joe Eula feels that Milton should have exercised even more control because the financially troubled Miller and the self-serving Strasbergs were on the prowl. Miller, in fact, with little income and enormous debts —alimony, child support, lawyers' fees, tax arrears—approached Milton about filing a joint income tax return with Marilyn and MMP. "Milton went over there and acted like the original Zanuck," claims Eula, "taking the family, spending money like a fool. Arthur saw that. Marilyn didn't give a shit, she couldn't have cared less, but Arthur cared. Those Strasbergs cared a great deal. They were 'protecting Marilyn from big, bad Milton.' Like hell they were, those fucking opportunists! They were doing a number on Marilyn."

The Millers were quartered in the far more grandiose Parkside House on ten landscaped acres with swans on a private lake and several resident servants. They had chosen country living to avoid the bumper-to-bumper traffic from London. From their respective houses, Milton and Marilyn could reach Pinewood Studios in under forty-five minutes on backroads.

Five days after his star arrived, Milton supervised her wardrobe and makeup tests for the Technicolor production. He chose one of those Edwardian costumes for her to wear to Terence Rattigan's welcoming ball in his country house at Sunningdale, a few miles from Parkside House. The gala affair, certainly the grandest of the grand parties the playwright was known for, included most of the great names of the British theater. They lined up in the garden, like presentees at a Royal Command Performance, to meet the radiant guest of honor poised with her husband beneath a rose-entwined arbor. Milton, you can be sure, had placed them there. As the evening simmered down and guests drifted away, Marilyn and her host waltzed on gracefully in the candlelit ballroom. If only Rattigan's "occasional fairytale," as he called *The Sleeping Prince,* had captured some of that magic.

One of the reasons Milton had chosen this Edwardian period piece for his partner was her figure. She had the perfect hourglass proportions so admired in that era—tiny waist, narrow back and shoulders, ample bosoms. Unfortunately, during filming, those proportions kept changing. "She would gain weight drinking champagne and eating to get through another wonderful weekend with Arthur," Amy groans. "Then, by Wednesday she had been given a diarrhetic so she was thin." Poor Beatrice Dawson, the designer, had to supply several facsimile costumes in different sizes to accommodate the expansible star. "I have two ulcers from this film," she disclosed, "and they're both monogrammed 'MM.'"

1

3

4

5

6

7

**1—10** When Marilyn married playwright Arthur Miller at the upstate New York home of his agent, Kay Brown, a select group of family and friends were invited to celebrate. Kitty Owens baked the wedding cake, topping it with the same bride and groom that Milton and Amy had used. Milton took the picture at the top right corner a few days before the wedding at Miller's Roxbury, Connecticut home.

8

9

10

"Bumble," as she was called, had been Amy's inspiration. On her first movie date with Milton, they had seen Anthony Asquith's film *The Importance of Being Earnest.* "Let's stay for the credits," she said. "I have to see who did those costumes." She tucked away the name of Beatrice Dawson and suggested it when the deals were made for *The Sleeping Prince.* The choice delighted Olivier, since the designer was a great friend of Vivien Leigh. "How did you know about Bumble?" he wondered.

"Because of *The Importance of Being Earnest,*" Amy told him.

"You're a good child," he said, and patted her on the head. His paternal solicitude sent shivers, far from familial, down Amy's back. Such Olivierian gestures usually affected women that way. That Devonshire cream voice, those vacant, velvety eyes, which had rendered Richard III the sexiest monster ever to corrupt a stage, worked just as well face to face. At the beginning they worked that way on Marilyn. He mesmerized her.

"I think if Arthur hadn't been around, Marilyn and Larry would have become lovers," Amy speculates. "She was thrilled with him at first and he needed a woman like that at that point in time, because it was the end of Vivien. He needed someone."

When filming started, however, confusion and antagonism came between them. She could not figure him out. When she was a good girl, he took it for granted. When she misbehaved, he ignored it. The paternal pats, the courtly affirmation that melted more secure women seemed merely patronizing to her. She wanted to get through to him, but she could not, because she was unprofessional in his mind and professionalism was where he lived. You arrived on the set on time with your lines perfect, your costume pressed, your hair combed ready to go. She did not work that way. She had never worked that way. She was not a disciplined actress. Her performance came when the camera rolled, not before. She needed film.

Olivier came to understand that, but his awareness would be a mixed blessing. "I hated her yesterday because she fluffed her lines, didn't look right, but I'm wrong," he told the Greenes as they watched the rushes one night. "The magic happens the minute you turn the camera on. This isn't acting. This is magic. She has it and I don't."

"Josh Logan, who had worked so wonderfully with her and with my mother in *Bus Stop,* warned Olivier not to kind of lord it over her," recalls Susan Strasberg. "He needed to be very direct and not confuse things too much, because she wasn't a trained actress in a certain way. My father had told him the same thing. And Olivier, of course, went and did the opposite. He was a wonderful actor, but he also had a very big ego and was very competitive, which he admitted afterwards, because, you know, whatever her problems were on the film, she makes it work and he's not too good in it."

Marilyn experienced emotional turmoil on and off the set during that English sojourn. Her month-old marriage was already tottering and her health was precarious. "During the first two weeks of that film she found the diary or whatever it was of Arthur's that spoke disparagingly of her," says Susan. "She was also having a lot of female troubles, which were excruciatingly painful." These might have been resolved by a hysterectomy, but because she wanted children she resisted. (Some accounts say she was pregnant and miscarried during the film, but Amy and Susan, among others, discount them.) Virtually isolated at palatial Parkside House, with nobody around but Arthur, who had betrayed her, Hedda, who drank and retired early, and Paula, whom one tired of very easily, Marilyn popped prescription pills and sipped champagne.

Such vicissitudes, even if he were aware of them, did not preclude professionalism for her director and co-star. His own imbroglios, which in many ways mirrored hers, certainly did not interfere. His fairytale

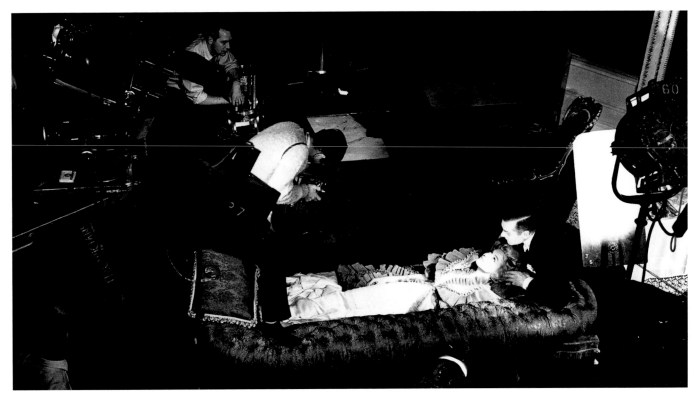

While filming *The Prince and the Showgirl* in England, Milton photographed Marilyn on the set with her partner, Sir Laurence Olivier.

marriage to Vivien Leigh was winding down in a welter of her recriminations and nervous breakdowns. The delicate balance had been further tipped by the casting of Marilyn in the role that Vivien had originated opposite her husband on stage. The fabled beauty was not thirty anymore. Marilyn was. Recently Leigh had quit a play saying she was pregnant, then supposedly miscarried. "She was decorating a nursery at their home, Notley Abbey, but it was all a ploy to get out of a play and give Larry what he wanted most, a child," claims Amy. "Vivien admitted to me that she never was pregnant and never had a miscarriage at that point in time, but just used it as a prop."

She also used Amy to cover her forays to Pinewood. "Come, we'll lunch on the set," she suggested on the telephone one morning.

"I don't want to go on the set," Amy demurred. "What's worse than having somebody's wife on the movie set?"

"No, no," Vivien insisted, "we'll lunch in the commissary."

"Well, let me see what they're shooting today and I'll call you back." Amy called Milton at Pinewood: "Vivien wants me to have lunch out there. You better check it out with Larry, because I'm not going to get in the middle of this."

"Good thought," Milton told her. He asked Olivier, who said, "Of course, if Vivien wants to come."

They lunched in the commissary, just the two of them. Nobody from the film showed up except Arthur Jacobs, MMP's publicist from New York. It was embarrassing for Leigh, but she should have known better than to be there. After lunch she said, "Come along, we're going to see the rushes." ("I realize she's using me, my tentacles are up. I'm smart enough to know they never show the rushes at midday," recalls Amy. "But it's Vivien Leigh, folks. I mean, this is Scarlett O'Hara. I'm not about to argue with her.") But, sure enough, they went to the screening room and sat through the rushes up to that point. She had arranged it with Cecil Tennant, Larry's agent.

The exquisite actress, who, besides Scarlett, had illuminated Blanche du Bois and Lady Hamilton, Anna Karenina, and Shaw's Cleopatra gazed intently at the screen, evaluating this celebrated upstart. She said nothing until they were leaving the screening room. "You know," she began, almost in a whisper, "I didn't think she would be that beautiful." ("And it broke her heart to say it," Amy laments. "It broke my heart to hear it, because I heard the tears deep inside.")

Olivier, meanwhile, had reached the boiling point with The Method and the Strasbergs: Paula on the set; Lee on the telephone. "Half the time her head was so full of the rigmarole of 'method,' her natural talent was suppressed," Olivier recalled. "She'd take ages over a shot, keep people waiting for hours." He would direct, she would listen, then look over at Paula, who would shake her head yes or no. If it was no, Marilyn would join her for a deep discussion of the whys and wherefores.

Often their exchanges led to transatlantic consultations with Lee: "I'll never forget the shock when she called my father hysterical and said, 'Lee, he wants me to be sexy.' Now, I'd like to think Sir Laurence Olivier said that humorously, but we'll never know." At one point, Marilyn even imported her New York analyst, Margaret Hohenberg, to audit her performance.

Finally, Olivier erupted. "If you ever do that again," he warned Paula, "I'll have you thrown off the set."

"You can't do that," she replied disdainfully.

"Try me," he said.

When she interfered as usual a short time later, he had two security guards physically pick her up and carry her off the set. Marilyn threw a fit. Olivier put his hands on her shoulders and looked into her eyes: "I'm the director of this film and I'm here to protect you. There's no discussion: You'll do as I say because you're

a professional. I'm not here to make you ugly or to make your voice squeaky"—he pitched his voice higher when he said, "squeaky," which sent her storming into her dressing room. She expected to find Paula waiting.

"Where's Mrs. Strasberg?" she asked a security guard.

"The car picked her up. She's on her way to London."

Milton appeared in time to bear the brunt of her fury: "How could you let him do this to me?" She ranted and raved for five minutes. He weathered the storm, then looked up with his cherubic face and said, "How'd you like to have Charlie Chaplin direct your next picture?"

*"What?"*

"You heard me. How'd you like Charlie Chaplin to direct your next picture?"

"I'd love it," she replied.

"Ok, let's get this thing over with." And she went back to work.

Paula would return, somewhat chastened, but a bigger problem remained. Amy describes it as she saw it:

Arthur began to show up every day in the dressing room and he was disruptive, because no matter what Larry told Marilyn to do, Arthur had an opinion about it. Finally one day Larry told him to get the fuck off the set or he'd have him thrown off. Now, this was Arthur Miller, folks. He still didn't have the sense or the pride to get out of Pinewood. I mean, what was he doing there? I went antiquing, I went to museums, anything to stay out of Milton's hair. He went back to her dressing room, they closed the door and sulked for the rest of the day. So Arthur was stirring the pot, because he knew it was a disaster between the two of them and he was hanging on for dear life. He knew that whatever idea he had in marrying her, it never materialized, and she felt the same. She was deeply unhappy because it was another failure in her life. And she couldn't talk to anybody but Milton and she didn't particularly trust him at that point because she knew, being a movie person, all he wanted was to get it in the can, bring it in under budget.

Hoping for a truce, Milton conceived a slight distraction for the feuding factions. He asked Cecil Tennant to arrange for the Millers to be presented to the queen at the Royal Film Performance, the annual charity gala at the Empire Theater. "Meeting the queen simmered everybody down for six weeks of preparation," recalls Amy, "because no matter what *Mister* Arthur Miller said, he was shitting in his pants with joy and anticipation that he was going to meet the queen." Coming on the heels of the London opening of *Bus Stop,* which garnered raves for Marilyn, the convergence of the monarch and the movie star created a stir with the British press and public. Marilyn's revealing gown did nothing to discourage it. In fact, her prominently displayed breasts made a big hit with the queen or, at least, with clamoring photographers as Elizabeth II surveyed them.

Following the royal diversion, it was friction as usual on the set. On good days, Marilyn knew that Milton had her best interests at heart. He took half a day to light her entrance into the embassy, and when she saw the rushes she shivered, actually shook. "I'm beautiful," she said. "Yes," Amy agreed, "because of Milton." And Marilyn leaned over and kissed him. She knew he was not out to get her. She knew Arthur was stirring the pot.

On bad days she thought everybody was against her and Milton had gone over to Olivier's side. When he tried to explain to her and her husband what her lateness was costing, she would whine, "Everybody's ganging up on me. Everybody's on Larry's side; nobody's on my side." Arthur, on the other hand, according to Amy, responded with something like, "What do you care? It's Warner Brothers' money." Milton, at the end of his bent, exploded.

"Schmuck!" he shouted. "It's our money!"

"What do you mean, it's our money?"

"MMP has x amount to spend on this picture. If we go over budget, we have to pay for it. It's out of our pocket. If you're late, if you waste time, if you shoot thirty takes, it costs us thousands of dollars." From that day forward, work proceeded on schedule.

For all its problems, *The Sleeping Prince* came in on time and under budget. When Milton handed Jack Warner the final accounting, there was $35,000 left over. He gave Warner a check.

"What's that?" wondered the studio chief.

"It's the money left over after all the bills were paid."

Warner smiled. "Keep it," he said. "You'll louse up my bookkeeping."

Milton went to the bank and had a check made out to Marilyn for the entire amount. "What's this for?" she asked. He explained and she wrote him a check for $15,000. He laughed and said, "You're still keeping more of the money." That was the kind of bantering, above-board relationship they had. But storm clouds were gathering.

Milton's angry exchange with the Millers before they finished the picture would have far-reaching consequences. When he had returned to Tibbs Farm that night and told Amy what happened, she shuddered. "You cut your own throat," she told him. "He'll never forgive you for that. Nobody calls Arthur Miller a schmuck." It was a prophesy, her Cuban intuition. And she was right. That moment marked the beginning of the end of Milton Greene's involvement with Marilyn Monroe Productions.

Warner Brothers retitled the picture *The Prince and the Showgirl,* which displeased Olivier. "It sounds like an Edwardian musical," he protested. The studio also did some cutting, which Marilyn blamed unjustly on Milton. This was the start of a concerted campaign to discredit her partner and wrest control of MMP. It seemed to be Miller's fine hand stirring the pot again, particularly as the company's officers, lawyers and accountants were replaced by his unqualified friends and relatives. With irrational fervor, Marilyn even tried to remove Milton's executive producer credit from their film. "When Marilyn married Arthur, it

1

4

2

5

6

3

**1+2** Marilyn poses for Milton's lucrative American Airlines aid campaign, Los Angeles, 27 February 1956.
**3** Milton shot Marilyn with Marlon Brando to promote an Actors Studio benefit, 1955.
**4** Marilyn hugs a discobolus in hairdresser Sidney Guilaroff's Hollywood home.
**5** Marilyn poses cheerfully with Olivier and Rattigan after signing them for *The Prince and the Showgirl*.
**6+9** In addition to their more formal sittings Milton often caught Marilyn unawares at Fanton Hill.
**7** Milton snapped this casual candid at the Los Angeles home of Joseph Schenck, 1953.
**8** Marilyn and Arthur Miller celebrate at the Westchester County Court House after obtaining their marriage license.

7

8

11

9

10

**10** When Terence Rattigan gave a gala ball to launch *The Prince and the Showgirl*, Marilyn arrived wearing an Edwardian costume from the film.
**11** The star makes her entrance for the Actors Studio benefit at the Astor Hotel in New York, December 12, 1955.
**12** Miller and Marilyn pose with a friend in happy times.

12

started changing and Milton was less and less a factor in her life," observes Jay Kanter. "She also became very dependent on the Strasbergs at that time and the relationship she had with Milton started to disappear. I don't know if she lost confidence in what he was doing or if she became suspicious of what he was doing. If she was, it was, in my opinion, not justified."

Milton blamed her husband and remained naively loyal to his partner. "I went through that split up with Milton and Marilyn, and it was tragic," attests Joe Eula. "Milton never believed what she would do, so he just sat there and did nothing about it. He never for one moment believed Marilyn would leave him, because he was really such a breadwinner for her, such a guiding light, such a foundation. The goddamned fool didn't understand that her husband had taken her away long before. Would you want your wife being owned forty-nine percent by somebody else?"

At the end of January 1957, two months after their homecoming, Marilyn returned to Milton's studio for a formal sitting. He arranged a series of black dropcloths to dramatize her simple red dress. The results were among their best, the quintessential Monroe-Greene creation—playful/provocative, innocent/wanton—without a hint of dissension or turmoil. In the final frames, with her body outstretched, her head turned away from the lens, she seems to be fading into an infinity of black. It would be their last session together.

The Millers continued their relentless campaign against Milton, Irving Stein and Joe Carr, MMP's accountant. Despite their insinuations, no evidence of foul play emerged, no indications of skullduggery. It was just personal, Miller's greed, Marilyn's need to trade one champion for another. "Marilyn wasn't dumb," states Michael Korda. "She realized that she didn't need Milton anymore. What did she need him for? Even without Arthur Miller she would have realized that." He had rescued her from studio slavery. He had given her the foundation from which to soar

as an actress. He had redefined her image with his lens, his "eye." She still needed him more than she knew, but it was a symptom of her greater need that she discarded him. Judy Quine discerns the deeper strains which made casualties of Marilyn's champions and ultimately of Marilyn herself:

> Milton gained a lot and then lost a lot. It was almost impossible not to have lost a lot if you became enmeshed in Marilyn's life. Her needs emotionally were impossible to fulfill. The person with more innercore strength usually goes into a relationship thinking they can help the person with less, but often the weaker one just drains out the equation so it comes down to that level. That was almost inevitable with Marilyn. I mean, there were well-meaning people in her life from time to time, but it could never be anything but a disaster, really, because she didn't have enough trust in herself to be part of a give-and-take, mutually concerned and caring relationship. I just don't think it was possible to sustain a relationship with her. It was too much emotional chaos. Her tragedy existed years before either DiMaggio or Miller or Milton met her. So people were stopgaps, little rest stops in the spiraling journey toward the end.

Milton and Irving Stein went to the offices of Miller's lawyers to negotiate the abrogation of his contract with MMP. They were greeted by Marilyn, Arthur, and a battery of lawyers gird for battle. When Milton told them he wanted only his investment back, roughly $100,000, they gasped. Miller, Amy says, spoke first: "That's all you want?"

"That's it. Whatever my investment was." They expected to be held up for millions, which someone inadvertently mentioned. "She knows that's not the way I operate," Milton replied, gazing at Marilyn.

"Take more," she whispered.

"No," he said, looking her in the eye. "Let me be the only one in your life never to take more."

Milton still thought his partner would come around. "Right up until the day he had to go to court out in

Milton captures Marilyn's highly erotic, yet playful, charm in the red
chiffon dress she wore at their last sitting in January 1957.

the Bronx and terminate the partnership, he never,
never believed she would go through with it," recalls
Eula. "When he came back, from that day on Milton
was a changed person. He was whipped."

The Prince and the Showgirl opened at Radio City
Music Hall in June. The reviews and the ultimate box-
office response were lukewarm, but in the passing of
time Marilyn's performance has come to be
considered, after Bus Stop, her best. The day after the
opening, however, the New York Times review echoed
the consensus: "The main trouble with The Prince and
the Showgirl, when you come right down to it, is that
both characters are essentially dull. And, incidentally,
the scene shown in the advertisements of Sir Laurence
kissing Miss Monroe's shoulder does not appear in the
film." That "scene" was actually from a formal sitting
with Milton Greene, based on a sketch by Joe Eula.

Given the chance, those two might have injected such
sensual shenanigans into the listless film.

Amy and Marilyn met for the first time in months at
the premiere. Amy was pregnant with her second son,
Anthony, and showing it. Marilyn came over, threw her
arms around her and kissed her. "Can I feel your
baby?" she asked, before placing her hands on Amy's
stomach.

"I don't think there were any hard feelings on her
part; I think there were hard feelings on my part,"
Amy reflects nearly forty years later. "I was so
disappointed in what she hadn't seen in Milton. She
didn't mean anything in my life one way or the other,
she meant something in my husband's life. I was never
jealous of Marilyn. Arthur was always jealous of Milton,
which is interesting in a way. Arthur had another life.
Why should he be jealous? I didn't need Marilyn

Monroe, but she sure as hell needed Milton Greene, and he needed her, because both of them were never the same after that. These two people should have been together through thick and thin. Nothing ...

nothing should have put them apart. I was smart enough to realize that. If Arthur had been smart enough to realize that, it would have been a whole other life for both of them."

Milton's provocative shot for *The Prince and the Showgirl* posters was not, alas, recreated for the film.

# THE BITTER END

"When you put so much of yourself into something and then it disappears, it's an emotional wrecking machine," says Jay Kanter. "To a large degree Milton became so totally absorbed in Marilyn's life and the whole idea of MMP that it was hard to go back to something he was so good at, which was being a great photographer."

Recoiling from the break he never thought would happen, Milton retreated into the depths of his "Russian gloom," drinking too much, taking too many pills. Usually happiest when working, he now considered his own work trivial and demeaning compared to his cutting-edge brush with picture-making. Those closest to him became concerned about the extent of his despair. "Nobody wants to admit it, but I'm here to tell you it scared the hell out of me," Joe Eula confesses. "That's one of the reasons I said, 'All right, buddy, come on, so you just got rid of one partner. I'll pick up where she left off. Let's go!' I figured he needed a help out; God knows he picked me up a few times when I was out. So we formed the Greene-Eula Corporation, and from that moment on

we rode the goddamned crest of the wave."

Milton purchased a charming, free-standing building on East Fifty-fifth Street, which became the bustling studio they shared. "Ten years of the greatest time of our lives," says Eula. Stars, models, props, Sally Kirkland's concepts, Eula's fantasies captured Milton's "eye" and filled his lens, yielding some of the most creative and memorable layouts in the last great years of *Life*. But Milton never quite relished it. "He never felt he was a success until the day he died," Eula discloses. "He had more covers than any photographer in the history of *Life* and came closer to achieving his dream then than he ever did with Marilyn. So, therefore, his dream was fucked up. He never could understand what his dream was. He said once that he was a failure because he hadn't made the millions. 'Just add up the $250,000s we had on those contracts,' I told him, 'and we've made millions.' But he equated it, somehow, with not being able to be the big Hollywood producer. He wasn't even qualified to do that shit. He was qualified to take pictures and that used to rankle him."

Michael Korda, a scion of England's foremost producing family, explains why Milton was doomed in the movie business from the start:

> Milton could never have kept MMP going. He didn't have the resources for it. Marilyn was too big a star for him to handle. Eventually all those studio guys wanted to know what they needed Milton for. Those were serious, heavy producers, tough. Milton thought he was tough. In a way he was as far as photographers go—you've got to be pretty tough to survive—but it's nothing compared to the way, let's say, Zanuck was tough.
>
> It was bound not to last, but the fact is he did bounce back. He did reemerge as a successful photographer. His problem was that he wanted to be a movie producer. He never came close. He was the fifth wheel on a large wagon named Marilyn Monroe. That's not being a movie producer. He was astute and shrewd, he knew all those people and could do certain parts of it, but you can't become a movie producer on the tails of having a contract with a big star, particularly with such a volatile and difficult star as the key to it.
>
> Marilyn didn't have too many friends in the business to begin with, so by attaching himself to her, I think he ensured a kind of closed war against him whenever he tried to do anything, because everybody resented Marilyn so much. By going to him in the first place she challenged the whole studio system, so Milton himself got tarred and feathered with the reputation.

It was an aspect of the spiraling-down effect induced by intimate contact with Marilyn. Despite his achievements with *Bus Stop* and *The Prince and the Showgirl*, Milton tacitly became persona non grata in the movie business. "There would be a lot of people who would have said, 'I don't want to let my client too close to Milton Greene, because he may do to my client what he did with Marilyn,'" speculates Jesse Rand.

Marilyn did not fare much better. She only completed three films after leaving Milton, all of them with directors on the preferred list he had drawn for her, only one of them a success. Billy Wilder's *Some Like It Hot,* a landmark comedy and a box-office bonanza, returned her to the delightful but one-note bimbo of her early Fox days. George Cukor's *Let's Make Love,* a big-budget bust made to satisfy her Fox contract, displayed none of that director's stylish wit or the star's extended range. It did, however, facilitate a torrid affair with the leading man, Yves Montand, as her relationship with Miller further deteriorated. The third film, John Huston's *The Misfits,* was a fascinating failure written by her husband. ("I'm always wondering," says Rand, "if their assassination of Milton was all a game to get *Misfits* going?") The picture, particularly as the last of both Marilyn and Clark Gable, has gained cult status over the years, but it remains a jumbled affair with Marilyn alternately touching and over the top.

It is worth noting that Paula Strasberg, often credited with Marilyn's *Bus Stop* and *Showgirl* achievements, coached her on these last three films without comparable results. Perhaps Marilyn herself discerned the missing ingredient when, in a fit of pique on *The Misfits* set, she reportedly screamed at Miller, "You've even taken away Milton, the only man I could trust."

Less than a week after completing *The Misfits,* the Millers announced from separate residences their impending divorce after four years of tenuous marriage. She had been closely associated with Milton for roughly the same number of years. Although the intensity and quality of sharing varied diametrically, both exchanges were propelled by a woman who, according to Susan Strasberg, "no matter where she got to, kept wanting to go further."

Milton was a visual talent who could have been a very good stage or film director, because what he saw in the camera nobody else saw. What he saw in Marilyn no one up to that time had seen. They mirrored Pygmalion and Galatea: she became the image that was in his head. She was pliable. She was willing. She would have done anything for him, because the two of them knew that secret. Nobody else knew the secret. Olivier glimpsed it when he saw her "magic" in the rushes, but Milton was the first to see it. Milton's perception of that magic, Marilyn's need to have it perceived, and the communion it inspired, that was their secret. Miller never saw it. "She never let Arthur in to see it, which is interesting," says Amy. "As far as that relationship goes, I think she wanted intellect and respectability more than anything else, so she married Abraham Lincoln, who was in her mind Arthur. I think it wasn't even a deep friendship, because they basically didn't like one another. It was a pact. You help me and I'll help you." Marilyn thought she was going "further."

Miller could never relax his own self-absorption long enough to understand his wife. Even his sprawling apologia written two years after her death became a glaring accusation. "I'll never forgive Arthur Miller, whom I idolized," says John Springer. "When he wrote After the Fall, it was as if he were saying, 'Fellas, I haven't written Death of a Salesman lately, but look what I had to go through.' He wrote about this vicious, drug-addicted, nymphomaniacal drunken broad, and it was as if he were writing about Marilyn, but none of her sweetness or vulnerability came into that character and that's what turned me off. He piously proclaimed later that he certainly didn't mean Marilyn. That's bullshit!"

Milton's bequest to the memory of his partner is more appropriate: images, still and moving images, lovingly lighted images, wistful, brash, innocent, sensual images, the illuminating documents of a collaboration that captured a woman and created an icon. "Probably the perception of people, if they have any perception of it, would be that Milton was someone exploiting a star," observes Don Murray. "It's just the opposite. He's somebody who was enhancing the career of a star and enhancing the creative gifts of a star. That was

obvious if anybody knew the situation. Just look at her career and her work before and her career and her work afterwards. I mean, the Milton Greene time was her best time."

Early in July, 1962, after four years without contact, Amy dreamt about Marilyn. She seldom dreams, especially not unpleasant dreams, but having been suckled by a Cuban witch, she is sensitive to all outside vibrations. When they awoke the next morning, she turned to Milton and said, "Marilyn needs you."

"What are you talking about?"

"In my dream, she's alone, she doesn't have anybody she can trust. She was sending me signals to tell you to go to Los Angeles."

"You know we're leaving with Sally Kirkland in three days to cover the Paris collections. I can't do that."

"Milton, for once in your life listen to what I'm saying. She needs your help. Get on a plane, don't take the assignment. Go and help her."

"Ok, I'll call her. And if she tells me she needs me I'll get another photographer to do the assignment." He called and said, "Amy had this dream ... "

"I've been thinking so much about the two of you," Marilyn interrupted. "It's incredible that Amy felt, not you, but she felt that I wanted to talk to you." And they talked for an hour and a half. She told him that she had been fired from another of those "Fox epics" with Dean Martin, but they were trying to get her back. "You know, I'm right back where I was before MMP. They're giving me the worst roles. It's like the last ten years never happened. I'm right back to where I don't want to be."

"Don't do it," Milton told her. "If you want me to come out there, I'll leave today. I'll cancel the Paris couture."

She backed down: "No, no, come on, you've already committed. Of course, I'll be all right. And, I'll tell you what, let's have a date when you come back in August." He spoke to her again before they left for Paris and everything seemed fine.

On Saturday, August 4, Amy and Milton dined with Marlene Dietrich and Alicia Corning Clark, "a nothing," according to Amy, "who married a much older millionaire who conveniently died on their wedding night." Clark said something derogatory about Marilyn, and Amy jumped to her defense: "What do you know? You don't know what this woman's been through. She's very unhappy and, who knows, she may end up killing herself and you'll feel very sorry for talking like that."

On Sunday, the Greenes had a picnic lunch at Fontainebleau. The phone was ringing when they got back to their room. It was Alicia Corning Clark, and in the most arrogant, know-it-all voice, she announced, "Your friend, Marilyn Monroe, just killed herself." Amy, dumbfounded, did not believe her. She handed the telephone to Milton, who talked to her for a while and then called Arthur Jacobs, the MMP publicist who had become a producer in Hollywood. Jacobs confirmed the story. Milton turned to Amy, his face drained of color. "You were right," he said. "I should have gone to her."

Milton never believed that she killed herself intentionally or, at first, that anyone else killed her. "She took sleeping pills, sipped champagne, then forgot how many pills she had taken," he maintained. "She didn't mean to do it." Later, as more evidence surfaced, he doubted that her death had been an accident at all. He felt perhaps others were involved. He never pinpointed the culprits, but took comfort from the notion that it had not been self-inflicted. It helped to dull his gnawing belief that going to her might have made a difference. Others, with the benefit of hindsight, believed that and more.

"Poor Marilyn, I feel so sorry for her," lamented Kitty Owens thirty-two years after Marilyn's death. "I think if she had stayed with Mr. and Mrs. Greene, and listened to them, I think she'd been well up the road now. I believe that. But, you know, sometimes you jes' don't do what you're supposed to do. What a wonderful world it would be if we did."

**FADE OUT**

Milton H. Greene

**PHOTOGRAPHS**

# ON LOCATION

They met in Hollywood at the end of summer, 1953, when *Look* magazine assigned their top photographer to shoot an up-and-coming sexpot. Over the next four years, during some fifty sittings, the abiding Monroe image emerged from their symbiotic, joyous collaboration.

Some of the most exuberant shots resulted from rambles around the standing sets on the Twentieth Century-Fox backlot with booty from the studio wardrobe department. She played the streetwalker in her *Bus Stop* blouse previously worn by Susan Hayward in *With a Song in My Heart,* a gypsy fortune teller, a simple peasant in Jennifer Jones's *Song of Bernadette* costume, and a rather bizarre saloon girl in an opulent chinchilla wrap and a jaunty boater.

Out in Laurel Canyon they took advantage of more rustic settings, and back in Connecticut they turned an afternoon in Richard Rodgers' swimming pool into a photographic romp. Without make-up or artifice, Marilyn gave Milton the girl behind the image.

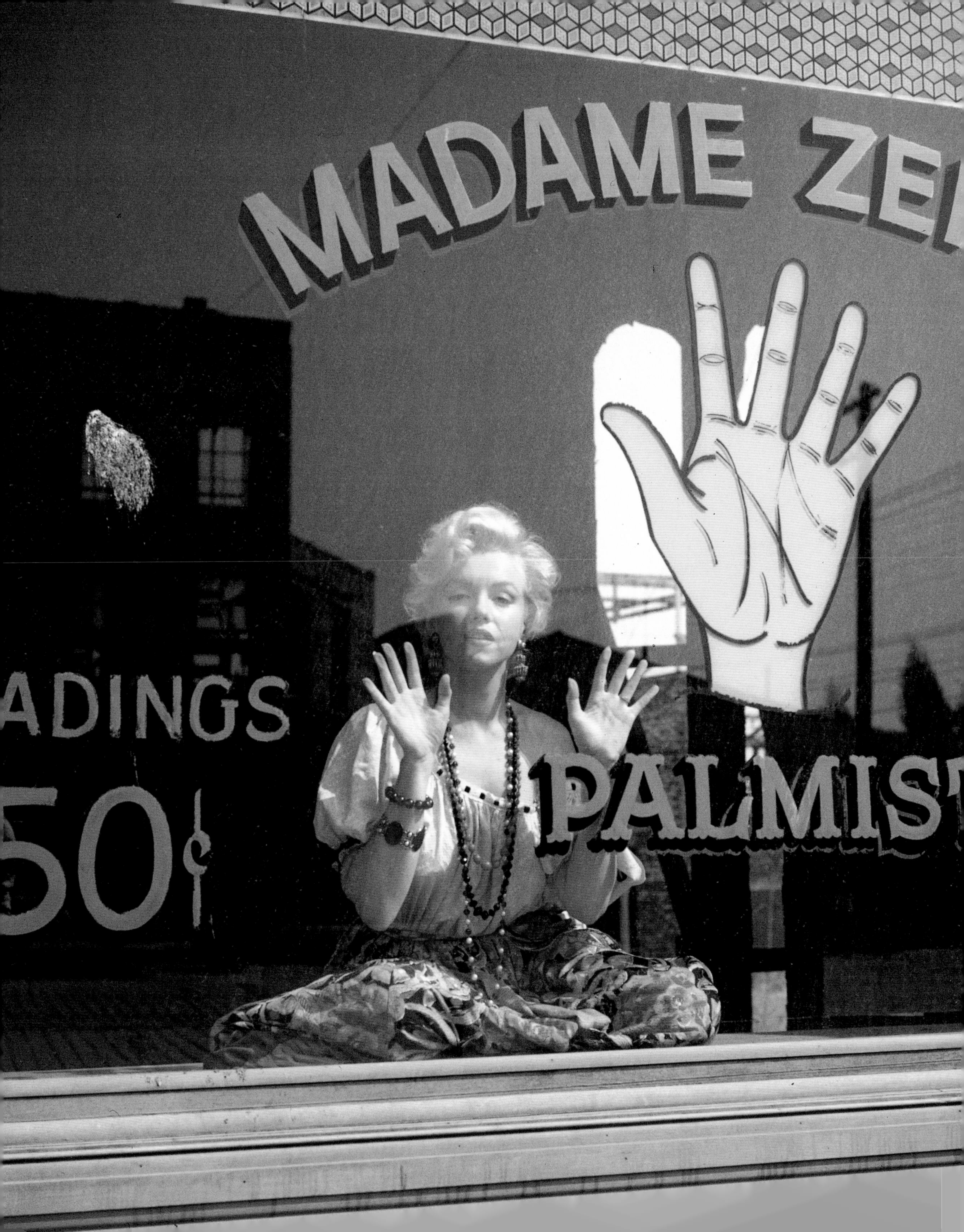

MADAME ZE
ADINGS
50¢
PALMIST

MILTON'S MARILYN

# IN THE STUDIO

It was in his studio that Milton could control and refine the images in his head, and from these more formal sessions the quintessential "Marilyn Monroe" emerged.

Their first sitting together in 1953, shot at Fox's portrait department, is represented on page 23 by one of the famous balalaika series that appeared in *Look* and in the frontispiece by a more personal portrait. The sweater was Amy's. The nudity, subtle but provocative, characterized their fruitful collaboration.

In the studio attached to his converted Connecticut barn, he captured her animating a couple of sweaters that Amy chose for her at a local boutique. During their sessions in his New York studio, Champagne and caviar relaxed the subject and yielded extraordinary pictures with such negligible props as a wicker chair, an ill-fitting dress with tulle underskirt, a white mink coat, and a simple red frock. The sitting in that red dress, shot in 1957, would be their last.

The so-called Black Sitting, photographed in New York before they left for California to make *Bus Stop,* remains the ultimate Monroe-Greene achievement. For all its sexy fishnet stockings and provocative attitudes, it retains the saucy innocence of a little girl playing dress-up. This subtle dualism, the essence of the Monroe image, explains her enduring appeal.

# ON SET

While performing the arduous tasks of a hands-on producer and mediator, Milton documented every aspect of the filming of *Bus Stop* and *The Prince and the Showgirl.*

From preparations on the set, to the star perfecting her love scene with leading man Don Murray or her artfully bad rendition of "Old Black Magic", to the dynamic portraits used in *Bus Stop*'s ads, the Greene camera captured it all.

Everything from costume fittings and lighting tests to the more sedate moments with Laurence Olivier on and off the set caught his eye during the tumultuous filming of *The Prince and the Showgirl* in England.

*Bus Stop* pages 173-205
*The Prince and the Showgirl* pages 207-219

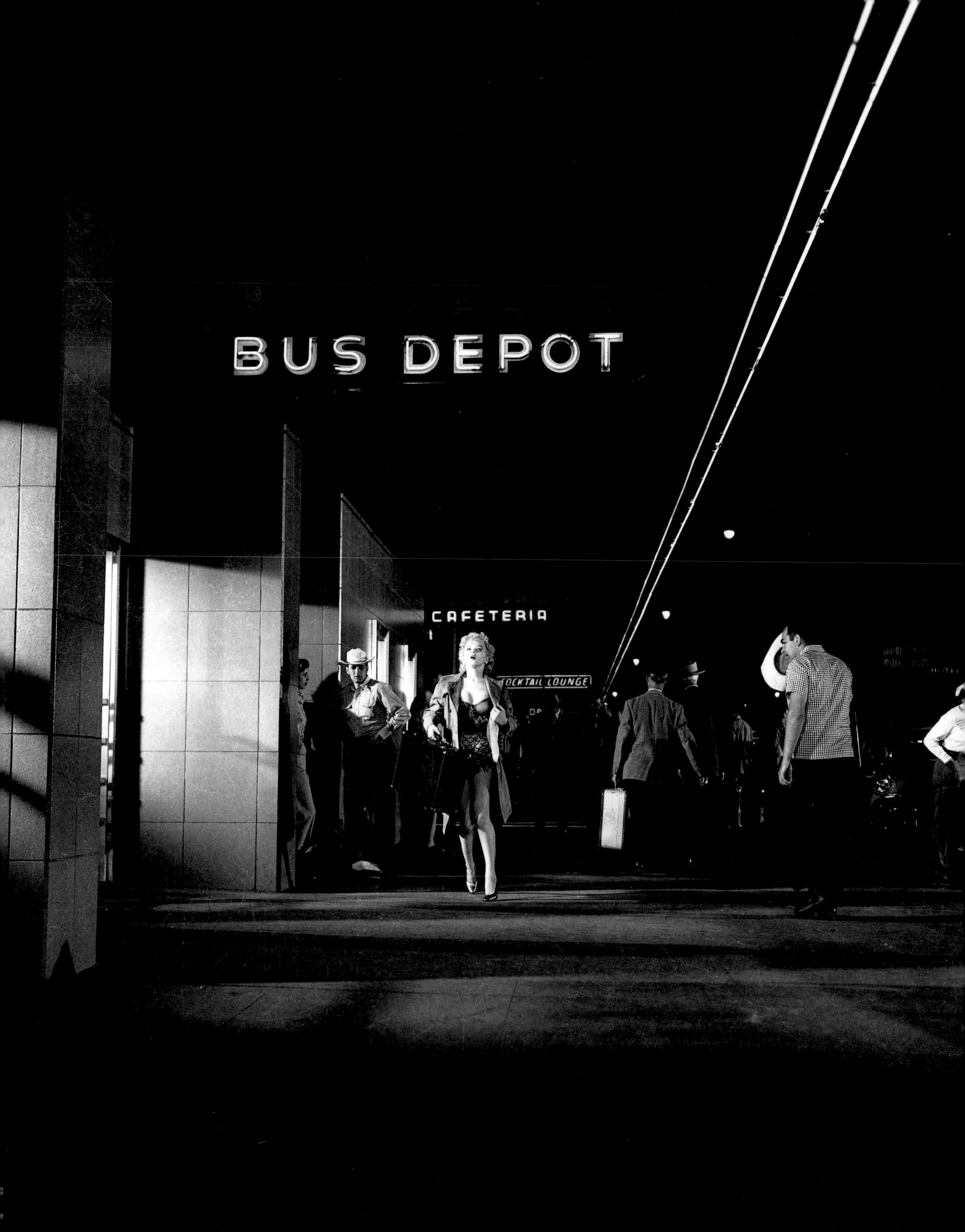
BUS DEPOT
CAFETERIA
COCKTAIL LOUNGE